W. H. G. Kingston

Exiled for the faith

W. H. G. Kingston

Exiled for the faith

ISBN/EAN: 9783743311176

Manufactured in Europe, USA, Canada, Australia, Japa

Cover: Foto ©ninafisch / pixelio.de

Manufactured and distributed by brebook publishing software (www.brebook.com)

W. H. G. Kingston

Exiled for the faith

Exiled for the Faith

A Tale of the Huguenot Persecution

BY

W. H. G. KINGSTON

AUTHOR OF
"CHARLEY LAUREL" "THE BOY WHO SAILED WITH BLAKE"
"A TRUE HERO" ETC.

LONDON:
THE SUNDAY SCHOOL UNION
57 AND 59 LUDGATE HILL, E.C.

CONTENTS.

CHAPTER		PAGE
I.	THE TWO COUSINS	9
II.	A WALK THROUGH PARIS	23
III.	THE VISIT TO THE ADMIRAL	34
IV.	WHAT NIGEL OVERHEARD	49
V.	UNDER WEIGH—ARRIVAL	61
VI.	NIGEL'S RETURN TO FRANCE	81
VII.	TREACHERY	103
VIII.	ATTACKED BY ENEMIES	122
IX.	PROCEEDINGS OF "THE INQUISITION"	140
X.	IMPRISONMENT AND RESCUE	162
XI.	CAPTURE OF THE FORT	180
XII.	CONCLUSION	194

LIST OF ILLUSTRATIONS.

	PAGE
HERETICS ON THEIR WAY TO PRISON	*Frontispiece*
MARY AND NIGEL	11
LIGHT AT EVENTIDE	37
HE DETERMINED TO APPEAR TO BE FAST ASLEEP	57
IN THE HEART OF THE FOREST	85
SEIZURE OF CAPTAIN BEAUPORT	115
CONSTANCE SAW AT A GLANCE THAT HE WAS NIGEL	131
THE BONFIRE OF BIBLES	155
THE FLIGHT	185

EXILED FOR THE FAITH

A TALE OF THE HUGUENOT PERSECUTION

CHAPTER I.

THE TWO COUSINS.

"AND what brought you to France, fair cousin?"

The question was put by a beautiful girl scarcely yet verging on womanhood to a fine intelligent youth, two or three years her senior, as they paced slowly on together through the gardens of the Louvre on the banks of the Seine, flowing at that period bright and clear amid fields and groves. Before them rose the stately palace lately increased and adorned by Henry II., the then reigning monarch of France, with its lofty towers, richly carved columns, and numerous rows of windows commanding a view over the city on one side, and across green fields and extensive forests, and far up and down the river on the other.

The walk along which the young people were proceeding was shaded by tall trees, the thick boughs of which kept off the rays of the sun, shining brightly on the gay flowers and glittering fountains, seen in the open space beyond them.

The young girl had the air and manner of a grown-up person, with that perfect self-possession which seems natural to those brought up in the atmosphere of a court.

Her companion's manner formed a contrast to hers; but though evidently not at all at his ease, as a brave man does when called upon to encounter danger, he had braced himself up to face those he might have to meet, who would, he naturally felt, look down on him on account of his travel-stained dress, his Scottish accent, and rustic appearance.

"In truth, Cousin Mary, I left Scotland as many of our countrymen are compelled to do, to seek my fortune abroad, and have come with letters of introduction to several noblemen and others; among them to Admiral Coligny, my father's old comrade in arms. Our castle is well-nigh in ruins, and my estate yields scarcely revenue sufficient to supply me with clothes and arms, much less to restore it as I wished to have done. I have already made two voyages to far-off lands, and come back no richer than I went, and have at length resolved to take service in the navy of France, in which I may hope

MARY AND NIGEL.

to carve out my way to distinction, with the help of the admiral."

"He may be ready enough to receive you and afford you his patronage; but I warn you, Cousin Nigel, that he may be less able to forward your interests than you may suppose. He is known to hold the principles of the leaders of those dangerous people the Protestants, who are hated and feared at court, where the Guises, the brothers of the Queen Regent of Scotland, have of late gained the chief influence. Take my advice, Cousin Nigel, seek some more profitable patron, and have nothing to do with the Huguenots."

"I thank you for your advice, cousin. I must confess, however, that I do not hold the opinion you express of the Protestants, but on the contrary, am greatly inclined to agree with their principles. I lately heard a wonderful preacher, one John Knox, who has appeared in Scotland, and brought thousands to see the gross errors of the papal system. He proves clearly that the Pope of Rome has no real ground for his pretensions to be the head of Christ's Church on earth; that he cannot be the successor of the apostle Peter, who never was Bishop of Rome; but that he is rather the successor of the great heathen high priest, whose idolatries he perpetuates and supports, and that therefore he and his cardinals and priests are impostors, who should on no account be obeyed. He clearly explains indeed that those who rule in the Seven-hilled city represent no other than the Scarlet Woman spoken of in the Apocalypse, their system being in truth the Mystery of Iniquity."

"Oh, dreadful!" exclaimed the young lady. "Why, Cousin Nigel, you are a rank heretic, and were you to express such opinions as these in public, your life would be in danger. Hundreds of Frenchmen have already been burned for holding opinions not half as bad as those you have expressed. I am almost afraid to listen to you; not that we trouble ourselves much about such matters at court, where people are allowed to think what they like, provided they do not utter their thoughts too loudly, or in the hearing of the doctors of the Sarbonne (the theological college of France), who have of late become rigidly orthodox, and are resolved to put down the reformers. I must advise you, at all events, to keep your own counsel; and if you are still determined to apply to Admiral Coligny, as your views agree with his, they will be in your favour."

"Thank you for your advice, sweet cousin," answered Nigel. "I will follow it so far as not to parade my opinions; but should they be attacked, I shall be ready, if necessary, to defend them either with my tongue or my sword."

"You are not likely to be called upon to use either of those formidable weapons, provided you are discreet," said the young lady, laughing. "You may occasionally at court hear the Protestants satirized, or made subjects of lampoons; but it would be folly to take notice of such trivialities, and you would be in continual hot water with worthy people, perfectly ready otherwise to treat you as a friend. I will speak to some I know, who will assist your object and forward you to the admiral, should you determine to seek his patronage."

"I would rather trust to so great and good a man than to any one else I have heard of in France," said Nigel; "and am anxious, as soon as possible, to make myself known to him."

By this time the young people had got within a few paces of the termination of the shady walk, when before them appeared a gay company of ladies and gentlemen, most of the former being very young, while the latter were, on the contrary, advanced in life, as their snowy locks and white beards betokened, though they were richly dressed, and were doing their utmost to assume a youthful and *débonnaire* manner. Nigel on seeing the gay company instinctively drew back into a recess by the side of the walk, unwilling, if possible, to present himself before them. His cousin being ready to humour him, placed herself on a garden seat, and invited him to sit by her. Perhaps she was unwilling that the interview with her near relative should be brought to an end sooner than could be helped. They could from this spot observe what was going forward without being seen. Merry laughter came from the party of gaily dressed people who passed along the walks, several approaching near enough to allow their features easily to be distinguished.

"Who are those?" asked Nigel, as several young people came slowly by, following a fair girl, whose beautiful countenance and graceful figure distinguished her from the rest, though many of her companions were scarcely less lovely. So thought the young Scotchman, as he stood watching them with admiring eyes.

"The first is our Lady Mary, about to wed the Dauphin of France," answered his cousin. "You must, as a loyal Scot, be introduced to her. Perchance if you are inclined to take service at court you may obtain a post, though his Majesty King Henry does not generally bestow such without an ample equivalent."

"My taste does not lead me to covet such an honour," said Nigel. "I should soon weary of having to dress in fine clothes and spend my time in idleness, waiting in ante-chambers, or dangling after the lords and ladies of the court. Pardon me, sweet cousin, for saying so. I came to France to seek for more stirring employment than such a life could afford. I will do my *devoir* to our young queen, and must then proceed on my journey to find the admiral. Had it not been for the packet of letters with which I was entrusted, as also for the sake of seeing you, I should not have come to Paris at all. But tell me, who are her Majesty's attendants? There is one whose countenance, were I long to gaze at it, would, I am sure, become indelibly fixed on my heart. What a sweet face! How full of expression, and yet how modest and gentle!"

"They are my two sister Maries, Mary Beaton and Mary Carmichael; * but it is neither of them you

* Three Scottish young ladies were sent over to France to attend

speak of. I see now; the damsel you describe is Constance de Tourville, whose father, by-the-by, is a friend of Coligny's. The admiral, I am informed, is staying with the count at this very time, and when I tell Constance who you are, she will, I am sure, find an excuse for despatching an attendant with you to her father. I can without difficulty make you known to her, as the etiquette of the court is not very rigid, or I should not have been allowed to wander about the gardens with a gallant young gentleman like yourself, albeit you claim to be my cousin and an old playmate."

"I see several gentlemen among the fair damsels, so I conclude that my presence is not altogether an irregularity," said Nigel.

"They are privileged persons, however," said Mary Seton. "That sickly youth who has just joined the queen and is awkwardly endeavouring to make himself agreeable is her affianced husband, the Dauphin. For my part I would rather not be a queen than be compelled to wed so miserable an object; but I am talking treason. Here comes one of the queen's uncles, the Duke de Guise—that tall, dark, ill-favoured gentleman. He is, notwithstanding, one of the most powerful men in France, and intends to be more powerful still when his niece and her young husband ascend the throne. But come; the party are moving on, and as Constance de Tourville is lingering behind, we can quickly overtake her, and when I have made

on Queen Mary. They were Mary Seton, Mary Beaton, and Mary Carmichael, and were named the Queen's Maries.

B

you known to her, you can tell her of your wish to see the admiral."

Nigel felt very unwilling to quit his hiding-place, but his cousin, taking him by the hand, playfully led him forward. They quickly overtook the interesting girl of whom they had been speaking. Nigel, as he was introduced, made a bow which would not have disgraced the most polished gentleman at court. The young lady smiled as she cast a glance at his handsome, honest countenance, with the glow of health on it, increased somewhat by the blush which rose on finding himself in circumstances so unusual to him.

"My cousin Nigel Melvin has come with an introduction to the admiral, who is, I understand, staying with your father, and he desires to set out to the château, though I would fain persuade him to take service at the court, instead of tempting the dangers of the sea, which he has the extraordinary taste to desire."

"Our house steward, Maitre Leroux, is at present in Paris, and will return to-morrow; and should your cousin desire his escort, I will direct him to await his orders," said the young lady in a sweet voice. "Where are you lodging, fair sir?"

"I arrived but this morning, and left my valise at L'Auberge de l'Ange," answered Nigel.

"I know not where that is; but Maitre Leroux will easily find it out, and will call for you at any hour you may name."

"A thousand thanks, lady, for your kindness," answered Nigel. "I gladly accept your offer, and shall be ready to set out at early dawn if the landlord will permit me to depart at that hour."

"Maitre Leroux will be at the palace this evening to receive a letter I am sending home, and I will direct him to call as you desire, though, as he loves his ease, he perchance may not be ready to commence the journey at quite so early an hour as you name."

While Constance was speaking, one of the ladies in attendance on the young queen turned back and beckoned to Mary Seton, who, hurrying forward, left Nigel with her friend.

"You will surely not take your cousin's advice, and seek for a post at this frivolous court," said Constance hurriedly, again looking up at Nigel's countenance. "Catholics alone are in favour, while the Protestants are detested. To which party do you belong?"

"I might say to neither, as I am not a Frenchman," answered Nigel, surprised at the young lady's question. "At the same time I have heartily abjured the errors of Rome."

"I am glad to hear it; I thought so," said Constance. "I myself am a Protestant. I am here on sufferance, or rather a hostage, and would gladly return to my home if I had permission. Persevering efforts have been made to pervert me, but I have had grace to remain firm to the true faith, and now I am simply exposed to the shafts of ridicule, and the wit and sneers of those who hold religious truth in contempt. You may be astonished at my thus venturing to speak to you, a perfect stranger, but I am sure that I may trust Mary Seton's cousin; and if you have the opportunity, I will beg you to tell my father or the good admiral what I say. I dare not write on the subject, nor can I venture to send a verbal message by Maitre Leroux."

"I faithfully promise to convey your sentiments to either one or the other," answered Nigel, casting a glance of admiration at the young girl, who could thus stand alone in her innocence amid the follies of that vicious and frivolous court. "As to accepting a place at court, even should it be offered me, I would refuse it, for my tastes lead me to seek my fortune on the wild ocean or in foreign lands; and it is with this object that I am about to visit the admiral, who will, I have been led to hope, forward my views."

"You cannot apply to a wiser or truer man in France," answered Constance. She was about to say more, when they were rejoined by Mary Seton, who came to conduct Nigel into the presence of the queen.

"As a loyal Scot you are bound to pay your *devoir* to her Majesty," she said. "Though neither of us have much recollection of our native wilds, we still regard our country with affection."

Nigel felt that there was no escaping, and mustering courage, went boldly forward till he reached the spot where the young queen was standing with several lords and ladies in attendance. Though unaccustomed to courts, he had too much native dignity to be overawed, and bending on his knee he lifted the hand of the young queen to his lips and reverently kissed it. Mary bestowed on him one of those fascinating smiles which in after years bound many a victim to her feet, and bidding him rise, questioned him about the affairs of Scotland, and various particulars regarding her lady mother the Regent, from whom he had been the bearer of a package. Nigel, gaining courage, replied discreetly to the young queen's questions. The Dauphin, however, made some remark which induced her to dismiss her countryman, when Nigel fell back to where he had left Constance, who had been rejoined by his cousin.

"You comported yourself admirably, and I congratulate you," said the latter. "You will, I am sure, after a little experience become a perfect courtier."

"I would not advise him to make the experiment," said Constance.

"There is little fear of it," answered Nigel. "I hope ere long to find myself on the wide ocean, where I may breathe the free air of heaven, which I much prefer to the atmosphere of a court; but I must crave your pardon, fair ladies, for showing a disinclination to live where I might bask in the sunshine of your smiles."

"That speech is truly worthy of a courtier," said Mary Seton, laughing. "Come, come, cousin, change your mind. Constance, you will help me to bring this gentleman to reason?"

"I would not attempt to influence him, even if I could," answered the young lady. "He has decided wisely. In your heart you know, Mary, that he is right; you yourself despise the miserable butterflies who hover round us with their sweet speeches, empty heads, and false hearts."

Constance de Tourville was continuing in the same strain, when the young queen, with her attendants and the other ladies and gentlemen of the court, was seen moving towards the palace, and she and Mary Seton were compelled to follow them. While Nigel was paying his parting adieus to the young ladies, a sigh escaped his cousin as he pressed her hand to his lips, for she knew the probability that they might not meet again. Her heart was still faithful to Scotland, and she loved her kith and kindred.

"Remember," said Constance, as he paid her the same mark of respect. "Be careful what you say to strangers; but you may trust Maître Leroux; he is honest."

CHAPTER II.

A WALK THROUGH PARIS.

ON reaching the gate of the palace, Nigel had met the captain of the Scottish guard, Norman Leslie, a distant relative, by whose means he had gained admission to the palace, and had been able to enjoy the interview with his cousin, Mary Seton.

"How fared it with you, Nigel, among the gay ladies of the court?" asked the captain, one of those careless characters, who receive their pay and fight accordingly, very little troubled as to the justice of the cause they support.

"I had a talk with my cousin, and had the honour of paying my *devoirs* to the queen," answered Nigel, cautiously. "Having now no longer any business in Paris, I am about to set out on a visit to Admiral Coligny. Can you direct me to my hostelry, at the sign of the Angel, and tell me where I can find a steed to carry me on my journey? for, albeit it would best suit my purse to trudge on foot, I would wish to present myself to the admiral in a way suitable to the character of a Scottish gentleman."

"As I am off guard I will accompany you, my good kinsman, and will assist you in procuring a horse," was the answer.

Nigel gladly accepted Leslie's offer, and the two Scotchmen set forth together. Nigel, being totally ignorant of the city, had no notion in what direction they were going. They were passing through the Rue St. Antoine, when they saw before them a large crowd thronging round a party of troopers and a body of men-at-arms, who were escorting between them several persons, their hands bound behind their backs, and mostly without hats, the soldiers urging them on with the points of their swords or pikes; Nigel also observed among them three or four women, who were treated with the same barbarous indignity as the men.

"Who are those unhappy people?" he asked.

"Heretics on their way to prison, to be burnt, probably, in a few days for the amusement of the king, who, ambitious of surpassing his sister sovereign, Queen Mary of England, and to exhibit his love for religion, manages to put to death ten times as many as she ventures to send to the stake, unless they recant, when they will have the honour of being strangled or hung instead," answered Leslie, in a nonchalant tone. "He and his counsellors are determined to extirpate heresy; but as the Protestants are numbered by hundreds of thousands, and as there are a good many men of high rank and wealth among them, his Majesty has undertaken a difficult task."

"I pray that he may alter his mind, or fail in the attempt," exclaimed Nigel, indignantly.

"I may whisper amen; although, as the foolish people bring the punishment on their own heads, I am not inclined to throw down the gauntlet in their cause, and must e'en do my duty and carry out the orders of the master whose bread I eat," said Leslie.

Nigel did not reply, but he felt more than ever determined not to take service on shore, however tempting the offers he might receive. Leslie told him that of late years, throughout France, many hundreds, nay, thousands of persons, after being broken on the wheel, or having had their tongues cut out, or being tortured in some other way, had been burnt at the stake for their religious opinions; but that, notwithstanding, the Protestants increased in numbers, and that, for his part, though himself a faithful son of the Church, he thought that a wiser plan might have been adopted.

"For my part, I believe that had not the Pope and the priests and monks interfered, and worked up some of our fanatic nobles and the ignorant populace to persecute their fellow-countrymen, they might have lived together on friendly terms; and, for the life of me, I cannot see why people should not be allowed to worship God according to the dictates of their consciences," added the shrewd Scotchman, with a shrug of his shoulders.

Nigel, who had only heard rumours of such proceedings, felt his blood boil with indignation, and instinctively touching the hilt of his sword, he vowed that he was ready to do battle in the cause of justice and humanity. His kinsman, who saw the act, smiled; and divining his thoughts, said, "Let me advise you to avoid interference in quarrels not your own, unless you receive a due recompense in pay, and then the less you trouble yourself about the rights of the case the better. Come along. The first thing we are to do is to look out for your steed. Honest Jacques Cochût will supply you with one which will bear you from one end of France to the other, and an attendant to bring the animal back. It will be more economical than purchasing a horse, unless you have a long journey to make."

Nigel accompanied his friend to the stables of Jacques Cochût, to whom Leslie was well known. A strong and active steed was soon engaged, with the promise that it should be ready at the door of the hostelry at an early hour next morning.

Leslie, leaving Nigel at the Angel inn, returned to his duty at the palace, while the latter, having ordered his supper, retired to his room to think over the events of the day.

It is needless to say that Constance de Tourville frequently recurred to his thoughts. He had heard enough to make him understand the dangerous position of the Protestants in France, even of the highest rank, and the fearful persecutions to which all classes were exposed. From the remarks Constance had made, it was evident that she herself was exposed to much annoyance, if not danger, even within the precincts of the palace, and he earnestly hoped that he might have an opportunity of speaking to her father, and obtaining her release.

He had sat for some time when he was aroused by a knock at the door, and the servant of the inn announced that a person desired to speak with him.

"Let him come in," said Nigel; and a respectable-looking man, somewhat advanced in life, as was shown by his silvery locks, stepped forward.

"I am attached to the house of the Count de Tourville, whose daughter despatched me to seek you out, and place myself at your service."

"Come in, my friend," said Nigel, offering him a chair. "You are, I presume, Maître Leroux, and I am grateful to the young lady for her kindness, of which I will gladly avail myself. Shall you be ready to set out to-morrow morning?"

"I had intended to do so, but business will keep me in Paris for another day," answered Maître Leroux; "and if you, fair sir, do not object to remain, I will gladly set forth with you at any hour you may name on the following morning. You may, in the mean time, find amusement in this big city of Paris."

Nigel, who was pleased with Maître Leroux, though anxious to continue his journey, willingly agreed to wait for the purpose of having his escort.

"But I have engaged my horse for to-morrow," he added.

"I will easily settle that matter with Jacques Cochût; and if you will accept of my company I will call for you, and show you some of the sights of our city, as you will, alone, be unable to find your way about the streets, and may chance to lose yourself, or get into some difficulty."

"Thank you," said Nigel. "I shall indeed be glad of your society, for, except a kinsman in the guards, I know no one in the whole of Paris."

These arrangements having been made, Maitre Leroux took his departure; and Nigel was not sorry, soon after supper, to throw himself on his bed, and seek the repose which even his well-knit limbs required.

Nigel, who slept longer than was his wont, waited at the inn some time for Maître Leroux. He was afraid to go out, lest the steward might arrive during his absence. At length his guide appeared.

"I have been detained longer than I expected," said Maître Leroux; "but monsieur will pardon me. We have still time to see much of the city."

They set out, and during their walk visited many places of interest, of which the steward gave the history to the young Scotchman.

"Your Paris buildings surpass those of our bonny Edinburgh in size and number, I must confess," remarked Nigel; "but still we have our Holyrood, and our castle, and the situation of our city is unrivalled, I am led to believe, by that of any other in the world."

"As I have not seen your city I am unable to dispute the point," answered the steward. "Would you like to visit one of our courts of justice? Though not open to the public, I may be able to gain admittance, and I am deeply interested in the case, albeit it would be wise not to show that, and having a stranger with me will be a sufficient excuse."

"Under those circumstances I will gladly accompany you," said Nigel.

They soon reached the portals of a large building, through which, after some hesitation on the part of the guards, the steward and his companion were admitted. Nigel observed that Maître Leroux slipped some money into the hands of two or three people, this silver key evidently having its usual power of opening doors otherwise closed. Going through a side door they reached a large hall, crowded with persons. Among those seated were numerous ecclesiastics, a judge in his robes, and lawyers and their clerks; while a strong body of men-at-arms were guarding a party of some fifty or sixty persons, who, from their position and attitudes, were evidently prisoners. They were men of different ranks; several, from their costume, being gentlemen, and others citizens and artisans. There were a few women among them also. All looked deadly pale, but their countenances exhibited firmness and determination.

"Of what crime have these people been guilty?" asked Nigel.

"Of a fearful one in the eyes of their judges," answered Maître Leroux. "They have been worshipping God according to the dictates of their consciences, and were found assembled together in a house at Meaux, listening to the gospel of the mild and loving Saviour. They have already been put to the torture to compel them to recant and betray their associates, but it has not produced the desired effect. In vain their advocate has pleaded their cause. Listen! the judge is about to pronounce their sentence."

Dreadful indeed that was. With blasphemous expressions, which cannot be repeated, the condemned were sentenced to be carried back to Meaux; fourteen, after being again put to the torture, were to be burnt alive in the market-place; most of the others were to be hung up by their shoulders during the execution of their brethren, and then to be flogged and imprisoned for life in a monastery, while the remainder were to receive somewhat less severe, though still grievous punishment.

The hardy young Scot almost turned sick with horror and indignation as he heard the sentence; and putting his hand to his sword, he was about to cry out and demand, in the name of justice, that instead of being punished, the prisoners should be released, when his companion grasped him by the arm, whispering, "Be calm, my friend; such events are so common in France, that we have grown accustomed to them. Hundreds have already died as these men are about to die; and we, their countrymen, have been compelled to look on without daring to raise our voices in their cause, or, as you are inclined to do, to draw a sword for their defence."

Maître Leroux, after exchanging a few sentences in an undertone with three or four people they met, whose sad countenances showed the interest they took in the condemned, led his young friend from the so-called hall of justice. On their way they looked into the magnificent church of Notre Dame. Priests in gorgeous dresses were chanting mass; music was pealing through the building, and incense was ascending to the roof.

"Impious mockery," muttered Nigel. "Well may Calvin and John Knox desire the overthrow of such a system, and desire to supplant it by the true faith of the Gospel."

"Hush! hush! my young friend," whispered Maître Leroux, hurrying him out of the church, regretting that he had entered it. "Though many may think as you do, it's dangerous to utter such opinions in this place."

"Can nothing be done to save these poor men?" asked Nigel. "Surely the king cannot desire the destruction of his subjects?"

"The king, like Gallio, cares for none of these things. He is taught to believe that the priests are the best supporters of his crown : and, at all events, he knows that they allow him full licence in the indulgence of his pleasures, which the Protestants, he supposes, would be less inclined to do."

"I would that I were out of this city of Paris, and away from France itself," said Nigel.

"Many think and feel as you do, and are acting upon it," answered the steward. "Already many thousand men of science and clever artisans have left, to carry their knowledge and industry to other lands; and others, in all directions, are preparing to follow. You will hear more about the matter when you visit the admiral, and my good master, who does not look unmoved on such proceedings. More on the subject it would not become me to say. Not long ago an edict was issued, by which all the old laws on heresy were revived, it being the resolution of the king to purge and clear the country of all those who are deemed heretics. Magistrates are ordered to search unceasingly for them, and to make domiciliary visits in quest of forbidden books, while the informer is to obtain one-third of the heretic's confiscated property. Should a person be acquitted of heresy in any ordinary court of justice, he may be again tried before an ecclesiastical tribunal, thus depriving him of all chances of escape. Even interference on behalf of a heretic is made penal, and should a person be suspected, he must exhibit a certificate of orthodoxy, or run the risk of being condemned. You see, therefore, young sir, that I am right in recommending caution as to what you say; not that these edicts have the effect expected, for Calvinism increases rapidly, and the stream of emigration continues from all parts of the kingdom."

They walked on in silence, Nigel meditating on what he had heard.

"Some fresh air will do you good after the scenes we have witnessed," observed Maitre Leroux. "We will take a turn in the Pré-aux-Clercs. It is but a short distance past the Invalides."

A WALK THROUGH PARIS. 33

It was evening, and a number of people were thronging that pleasant meadow on the banks of the Seine, the Hyde Park of that period. A party of young men coming by struck up one of the hymns of Marot, a translation of one of the psalms of David, written some years before by the Protestant poet. Others joined in, and evidently sang them heartily; several other parties, as they passed along, were indulging in the same melodies.

"How is it, after what you have told me, that the people venture to sing these hymns?" asked Nigel. "I know them well, for they have already been introduced into our Protestant congregations in Scotland."

"They became the favourites of the king and court before they had the significance they now possess," answered the steward; "and it is only thus that many who hate the papal system can give expression to their sentiments. Before long, however, I fear that they will be prohibited, or those who sing them will be marked as suspected. Alas, alas! our lovely France will be deprived of all freedom of thought, opinion, and action."

The worthy Maître Leroux seemed greatly out of spirits as they took their way back to the inn. They parted at the door, for Nigel felt no inclination to go forth again, and the steward had business, he said, to attend to. He promised to call for Nigel at an early hour the next morning to set out for Meaux, undertaking to direct Jacques Cochût to have his horses in readiness.

CHAPTER III.

THE VISIT TO THE ADMIRAL.

AÎTRE LEROUX did not call at as early an hour as Nigel expected. His own horse and attendant had been at the door for some time before the steward made his appearance. He had an ample apology to offer, having been employed in an important matter till late at night.

"Come," he said, "we will make up for it. The lateness of the hour matters not, for, with your permission, we will halt on the road, so as to arrive early at the château to-morrow."

They set out, followed by their two attendants. After leaving the gates of Paris they continued some distance along the banks of the Marne. The road was rough in places, and often deep in dust; full of holes and ruts in others, which made it necessary for the riders to hold a tight rein on their steeds, and prevented them generally from going out of a walk.

Maitre Leroux carried a brace of huge pistols in his holsters, while Nigel had a sword and a light arquebus, both their attendants being also armed; so that they were well able to defend themselves against any small party of marauders such as infested the roads in the neighbourhood of the capital.

"We must make but a short stage to-day," said Maitre Leroux. "In truth, I am unwilling to travel late in the evening, and prefer stopping at the house of a friend to taking up our quarters at an inn where we might meet with undesirable companions."

"But I shall be intruding on your friend," said Nigel.

"Pardon me; you will, on the contrary, be heartily welcomed. I am very sure of your principles, and they agree with those of our host and his family, so you need not be under the restraint which would be necessary were we to sleep at a public inn."

These arguments at once overcame any scruples Nigel might have felt at going to a stranger's house uninvited.

It yet wanted a couple of hours to sunset when they reached a good-sized mansion, though not possessing the pretensions of a nobleman's château. The owner, a man advanced in life, of gentlemanly refined manner, received Maitre Leroux in a friendly way, and on hearing from him who Nigel was, welcomed him cordially. Nigel was conducted into a saloon, where he was introduced to his host's wife and daughters and several other members of the family. Supper was quickly prepared, and Nigel found himself at once at home.

As soon as the meal was over several other persons came in, some apparently of the same rank as the host, and others of an inferior order, but all staid and serious in their demeanour. The doors and windows were then carefully closed, and Nigel observed that two of the party went out armed with swords and pistols, apparently to watch the approach to the house.

A large Bible was now produced, and several of the party drew forth smaller editions from beneath their garments. The host then offered up a prayer, and opening the Bible, read a portion, commenting as he proceeded. A hymn was then sung and more of the Scriptures read, after which the host delivered an address full of gospel truth, while he exhorted his hearers to hold fast to the faith, but at the same time remarked that they would be justified in flying from persecution if no other means could be found of avoiding it at home. He reminded all present, however, that their duty was to pray for their persecutors, and however cruelly treated, not to return evil for evil. Nigel was reminded of various meetings of the same character he had attended in Scotland, where, however, every man could speak out boldly, without the fear of interruption which seemed to pervade the minds of those present. He now knew that his host was one of the many Protestants existing in the country who ventured thus in secret to worship God according to their consciences, even though

LIGHT AT EVENTIDE.

THE VISIT TO THE ADMIRAL.

running the risk of being condemned to death as heretics.

After the guests had retired, the family spent some time in singing Marot's hymns.

"Ah!" said the host, "it is only in praising God and reading His blessed words that we can take any pleasure. It is our consolation and delight, and enables us without complaining to endure the sad condition to which bigotry and tyranny have reduced our unhappy country. The only prospect now before us is exile, or imprisonment and death."

Nigel answered without hesitation that he felt much satisfaction in again having the opportunity of worshipping, as he had been accustomed to do at home, according to his conscience, and hearing the Bible read and faithfully explained.

His host wishing him and his companion a friendly farewell, and expressing a hope that he should see him again, they took their departure at an early hour the next morning.

They had proceeded some distance when they entered a forest, through the centre of which the high road passed. They had been pushing on rather faster than usual, Maitre Leroux being anxious to get through it as soon as possible, when they saw before them a body of soldiers. As they got nearer they found that they were escorting a number of prisoners seated in rough country carts, into which they were fastened with heavy chains.

"Who are these unhappy people?" inquired Nigel.

"The same we saw condemned in Paris," answered Maître Leroux with a sigh. "If we do not wish to share their fate we must exhibit no sympathy for them, as the wretches who have them in charge would rejoice to add to their number. As it will be impossible to pass them at present, we will drop slowly behind."

"Would that I had a band of Protestant Scots with me, we would soon set them at liberty!" exclaimed Nigel.

"Hush, hush! my friend," whispered the steward; "it becomes us not to fight with carnal weapons; such is Dr. Calvin's advice."

Just at that moment a voice exclaimed, "Brethren, remember Him who is in heaven above!"

Some of the rear guard immediately turned round, and with drawn swords dashed furiously towards Nigel and Maître Leroux, believing, evidently, that one of them had uttered the exclamation they had heard. They both drew up, for flight would have been useless, when, just as the troopers had got some fifty yards from them, a man advanced from among the trees and repeated the words in a loud tone. He was instantly seized by the soldiers, and being dragged back along them, was thrown into one of the carts among the other prisoners. His appearance probably saved the lives of Nigel and his companion, for the doughty Scot had drawn his sword, and would have fought desperately before he would have yielded himself a prisoner.

"Pull in your rein, I entreat you," said the

steward; "we must not turn round, and the sooner we let these people get to a distance from us, the better."

Nigel, seeing that it would be hopeless to attempt assisting the unfortunate man, did as his companion advised, and they accordingly waited till the troopers were out of sight, taking good care not again to overtake them. Their progress was thus considerably delayed, and not till they came to a road passing outside the town of Meaux did they again venture to push forward.

They managed before sunset to reach the Château de Tourville, a high conical-roofed pile, with numerous towers and a handsome gateway. Maitre Leroux, conducting Nigel to a waiting-room near the entrance, went at once to the count, taking his letter of introduction. Nigel had not been left long alone when the steward returned with the request that he would accompany him to the hall, where, he told him, he would find the count and admiral with several other persons. Nigel, not being troubled by bashfulness, quickly followed his guide.

The count, who was of middle age and handsome, courteously rose from his seat at the top of the table to welcome him. At the right hand of the count Nigel observed a person of middle height, ruddy complexion, and well-proportioned figure, with a calm and pleasant, if not decidedly handsome countenance. On the other side sat a tall man, whose sunburnt features, though regular, wore an expression which at the first glance gave Nigel the feeling that he was not a person in whom he would place implicit confidence, though directly afterwards, as he again looked at him, his manner seemed so frank and easy, that the impression vanished. Several other persons of different ages, and apparently of somewhat inferior rank, sat on either side of the table.

"Which of those two can be the admiral?" thought Nigel; "the last looks most like a naval commander."

"The Lady Mary Seton, your cousin, and my daughter, have written in your favour, young sir, and I am glad to see you at the château; you have, I understand, also a letter of introduction to Admiral Coligny, to whom allow me to make you known." Saying this, the count presented Nigel to the gentleman on his right side, who requested the person next him to move further down, bidding Nigel to take the vacant seat.

Nigel observed that the meal was over, but the count ordered the servant to bring in some viands for the newly arrived guest.

"As I take no wine you will allow me to read the letter brought by this young gentleman," said the admiral, turning to the count; "I never defer looking at an epistle if it can possibly be helped."

The count bowed his acquiescence, and the admiral quickly glanced over the letter which Nigel had presented to him.

"I shall be glad to forward your object," he said, turning round with a calm smile, and playing with a straw, which he was wont to carry in his mouth.

"Fortunately, I have an opportunity of doing so. I am about to fit out an expedition to form a settlement in the southern part of America, and if your qualifications are such as I am led to believe, I will appoint you as an officer on board one of the ships. You will have but little time to remain idle in France, as we wish the ships to sail as soon as the emigrants who are going on board them can be collected. They will undoubtedly be anxious without delay to leave our unhappy country, where they are constantly subjected to the cruel persecutions of their opponents in religious opinions. Would the service I propose suit your taste?"

"Though I might wish to engage in some more warlike expedition, yet I am willing and glad to go wherever you, sir, may think fit to send me," answered Nigel.

"Well spoken, young man," said the admiral. "War is a necessity which cannot be avoided, but there are other employments in which a person may nobly engage with far greater advantage to himself and his fellow-creatures. Such is the work in which I desire to employ you—the noble undertaking of founding a new colony, and planting the banner of pure religion and civilization in the far-off wilds of the Western world."

The admiral spoke on for some time in the same strain, till Nigel felt inspired with the same noble enthusiasm which animated the bosom of the brave and enlightened nobleman who was speaking to him.

Many questions were put to him concerning his

nautical knowledge and religious belief, to which he answered in a satisfactory manner.

"I believe you are well suited for the undertaking, and I will forthwith make you known to the commander of the expedition, my friend Captain Villegagnon," said the admiral.

The dark man Nigel had remarked, hearing his name mentioned, looked toward him. Nigel bowed. The admiral, after explaining Nigel's qualifications, went on to inquire what posts were vacant in the squadron?

"That of the second officer on board my own ship, the *Madeline;* and I shall be pleased to have a seaman of experience to fill it, although he is not a native of France," answered the captain.

"You may consider your appointment as settled, my young friend," said the admiral. "I will desire my secretary to make it out, and as you assure me that you are a true Protestant, I willingly appoint you, such being the religious opinions of all those who are about to form the colony of Antarctic France, which I trust will be well-established under the wise government of Monsieur Villegagnon. Many other ships will sail forth with emigrants seeking an asylum from the persecutions they are subjected to in France on account of their religious opinions."

Nigel warmly thanked the admiral for the prompt way in which he had met his request.

"Say nothing about that, my young friend; we are too glad to find Protestant officers ready to engage in the expedition," was the answer.

THE VISIT TO THE ADMIRAL. 45

The conversation now became general, and the plans for the future colony were freely discussed, the count, who appeared as much interested as the admiral, taking a leading part—indeed, Nigel gathered from what he heard, that he himself intended to go out among the first colonists.

The idea of establishing the colony had been started, so Nigel understood, by Monsieur Villegagnon, who had chosen the Bay of Nitherohy, since known as that of Rio de Janeiro, as the site of the first town to be built. It was a place which he had visited some years before on a trading voyage, when he and his companions had been well received by the natives, though they were at enmity with the Portuguese, already established in the country, who claimed it as their own. This latter circumstance Monsieur Villegagnon remarked was of little consequence, as they were few in numbers, and, with the assistance of the natives, could easily be driven out.

The repast being over, the admiral rose from the table, the other guests following his example. Calling to Captain Villegagnon, he took him and Nigel into the deep recess of a window to have some further conversation on the subject of the proposed colony.

"Monsieur de Villegagnon sets out to-morrow to take command of the squadron, and you will do well to accompany him, young sir," he said, turning to Nigel. "You will thus be able to superintend the fitting out of your ship, and see that the stores come on board, and that proper accommodation is prepared for the emigrants; many are of rank and position in society, and there are merchants, soldiers, and artificers, and you will have to consider how best to find room for them. I am glad to say that the king himself takes great interest in the success of the colony, and under the able management of so skilled a leader as he who has been appointed to the command, we may hope that the flag of France will wave proudly ere long over many portions of the continent."

"It will not be my fault if the noble enterprise fails to succeed," said the captain, drawing himself up proudly, and then bowing to the admiral in acknowledgment of the compliment. "My chief satisfaction is, however, that a home will be found for so many of the persecuted Protestants who are compelled for conscience sake to leave their native land."

"You are right, my friend; that is a noble sentiment," observed the admiral; "and I would urge our friends who are dissatisfied with the state of affairs at home to place themselves under your command."

"From the expressions our host has uttered, I may hope that he also will render valuable aid to our undertaking," observed the captain.

"No one, be assured, more warmly enters into our views," answered the admiral, "and he will both with his purse and influence assist us, if he does not do so in a more effectual way."

They were soon after joined by the count, who requested the captain to reserve two cabins for some persons who intended going on board just before the squadron put to sea.

From the conversation which ensued, Nigel found that most of the persons present purposed joining the expedition. They were all, he found from the remarks they made, Protestants, and haters of the system of persecution which had so long been the curse of France. Most of them had already disposed of their possessions, and were only waiting till the squadron was completely equipped to go on board. Among them was a Protestant minister, and, notwithstanding the edicts against meeting for public or private worship, the doors of the château being closed, before retiring to rest all the inmates were collected, the Bible was read and prayers offered up, those for the success of the undertaking and the preservation of the persons about to embark not being forgotten.

Maitre Leroux accompanied Nigel to his chamber. He expressed his pleasure on hearing that he had obtained the object of his wishes.

"Would that I could accompany you," he said, with a sigh; "but my duty compels me to remain, and watch over my master's property, should he be called away. Ah, he is a kind, good master, and his daughter is an angel. I would lay down my life for her sake, should she be deprived of her father—and we never know what may happen in these times. Alack! I fear that she is in society little congenial to her taste and opinion, for she is a true Protestant, as was her sainted mother, now in heaven."

Nigel felt deeply interested in listening to the garrulous steward's account of his young mistress, and encouraged him to go on. She had been compelled, against her father's and her own wish, to reside at court, for the evident purpose of perverting her faith ; "but she is too sound and too wise to allow them to succeed," he added, " though I would the dear young lady were back with us again."

CHAPTER IV.

WHAT NIGEL OVERHEARD.

ALL arrangements having been made, the next morning, shortly after the sun had risen, Captain Villegagnon, with a considerable party, were ready to set out for Havre de Grâce, the port at which the squadron was fitting out.

They purposed to avoid Paris, but had to pass through Meaux on their way to join the high road leading to Havre.

The good admiral and Monsieur de Tourville came out to wish them farewell as they mounted their horses, and Maître Leroux was waiting at a little distance, where he might have a few last words with Nigel.

"Farewell, my young friend," he said, putting a small Testament into his hand; "you will find this an inestimable treasure. I dare not keep it long, as it is considered treason for a Frenchman to possess God's Word, though I have hidden away another copy to which I may go when unobserved to refresh my soul; and, mark you, should my master and young mistress ever have occasion to seek for your assistance, you will, I am sure, afford it."

"I promise you that I will most gladly," answered Nigel, wondering what the old steward could mean. Wishing his worthy friend good-bye, he pushed on to overtake his travelling companions.

On entering Meaux, they found the town in a strange commotion, the people all rushing with eager looks to the market-place, in which, as they reached it, they found a large crowd assembled. They caught sight of a number of high gibbets erected at intervals round it, while in the centre was a circle of stakes surrounded by faggots. The travellers would have passed on, but the dense crowd prevented them from moving, and their leader himself showed no inclination to press forward.

Presently shouts arose, and, the crowd opening, a horse was seen dragging a hurdle, on which a human being lay bound, the blood flowing from his mouth. A party of soldiers next appeared with a number of persons, their hands bound behind them, in their midst; while priests, carrying lighted tapers, were seen among them, apparently trying to gain their attention. Some of the prisoners were singing a hymn of Marot's, and all carried their heads erect, advancing fearlessly to the place of execution. On arriving, they were seized by savage-looking men, while some were speedily hoisted up to the gibbets by their shoulders, where they hung, enduring, it was evident, the greatest agony. Fourteen of the party were then bound to as many stakes, the unhappy man on the hurdle being the first secured. Among them Nigel recognized the person who had been seized in the forest on the previous day for shouting, "Brethren, remember Him who is in heaven above." Though the cords were drawn so tight as to cut into their wrists and ankles, no one uttered a cry for mercy, but, lifting their eyes to heaven, continued singing, or exhorting their companions to be firm.

The faggots being now piled round them, the priests retired, uttering curses on their heads; while bands of music struck up to drown the voices of the sufferers. At the sight of two men approaching with torches, the people raised loud shouts of savage joy, and one of the piles of faggots surrounding the stake, that to which the chief person, whose tongue had been cut out, was bound, was speedily kindled.

"All! all! Let them all be burned together," shouted the mob, dancing frantically.

The other piles were quickly lighted, the smoke ascending from the fourteen fires forming a dark canopy overhead.

The victims, as long as they could be distinguished, were seen with their eyes turned to heaven, singing and praising God with their last breath.

The savage fury of the ignorant populace was not yet satiated. Those who had been hung up by the shoulders were now taken down, and so dreadfully flogged, that some of them petitioned that they might be thrown into the flames amid the ashes of their martyred friends; but this was a mercy their cruel executioners had no intention of affording them. Bleeding, they were dragged off to be imprisoned in a monastery, where they were to be shut up for life.

At length Villegagnon, who had looked on with perfect indifference, called to his companions to follow, and, the crowd beginning to disperse, they were able with less difficulty to advance.

The lowest of the rabble only had exulted in the dreadful scene; the greater number of the people exhibited very different feelings. Nigel observed many in tears, or with downcast looks, returning to their homes; others exchanging glances of indignation; and he heard several exclaiming, "They died in a righteous cause. May we have grace to suffer as they have done."

"Truly, as I have heard it said in Scotland, 'The blood of the martyrs is the seed of the Church,'" observed Nigel to another of his companions, whose tears and groans showed the grief he suffered at the spectacle he had just witnessed.

Villegagnon kept his party together, for more than once some of the more ferocious persons of the mob cast suspicious looks at them, and mutterings arose, "Who are these? They have the air of

Lutherans, or they would look more joyous at the destruction of heretics."

"I hold the king's commission, and these are under my orders," cried Villegagnon. "Make way, good people, make way, and allow us to proceed on our journey."

Still the mob pressed round, and where showing a determination to stop the travellers, when a monk stepped forward, and exclaimed, "I know that gentleman, and he is a true son of the Church. Interfere not, at your peril, with him and his companions."

Nigel fancied that he observed glances of intelligence exchanged between the captain and the monk, who had so opportunely come to their rescue. The mob, at length pacified, drew back, and the party were allowed to leave the town without being again molested.

They pushed on as fast as their horses could go.

"We have had a happy escape," observed Nigel's companion, "for although a large portion of the population of Meaux are Protestant, yet the rabble, supported by the troops and some of the government authorities, have the upper hand, and it would have fared ill with us had we been stopped and our object discovered."

Night had already set in when they reached a hostelry where they were to remain till the morning. As most of the travellers were fatigued, they retired to rest as soon as supper was over, with their saddles as pillows, and their cloaks wrapped round them, lying down in the chief saloon, wherever space could be found. Nigel, with two or three others, sat up some time longer, when, having got his saddle and cloak, intending to seek repose, he found every place occupied. While hunting about, he entered a small room in which were a couple of truckle bedsteads. Neither was occupied.

"I am in luck," he said to himself, and placing his saddle and other property by his side, having taken off his riding boots and some of his clothes, he threw himself upon one of the beds which stood in a corner.

Drawing the coverlid over him, he was soon, sailor-like, fast asleep. After some time, he was awakened by hearing the door open, and, looking up, he saw two persons enter the room. One was Villegagnon, who carried a lamp in his hand; the other was, he saw by the person's costume, an ecclesiastic. They advanced across the room towards the window, where stood a table and a couple of chairs. Villegagnon threw himself into one of them, with his back towards him, the other imitating his example. The latter produced writing materials, and several papers, which Villegagnon held to the lamp to read.

"You have made a happy commencement of your work, my friend," said the priest. "If you carry it out thoroughly, the Church, the Duke of Guise, and the Cardinal of Lorraine will be deeply indebted to you. Twenty Calvinist nobles, and some four score of the commonalty, have, I see, determined to accompany you, and they will entice many more. We shall be glad to be rid of them at present out of France, and we will then send out a larger number of faithful Catholics, so that you will reap the honour of founding a French colony in the New World, the Church will triumph, and the Calvinists be extirpated."

"But the proceeding smacks somewhat of treachery, and it can matter but little to you at home whether the colony is established by Calvinists or Catholics, so that it is firmly grounded and adds to the honour and glory of France," observed Villegagnon.

"Nay, nay, my friend," said the priest, putting his hand on the captain's arm; "remember that the means sanctifies the end. We can allow no Calvinists to exist, either here or abroad. They would be continually coming back with their pestiferous doctrines, or, finding themselves in the majority, would speedily put an end to our holy Church. They must be extirpated, root and branch."

"I have no wish to support the Protestants, as thou knowest right well, reverend father," answered the captain; "but they are countrymen, and fight well, and labour well, and count among their number the cleverest mechanics in France. I know not how it is, but it seems to me that everywhere the most intelligent men have become Calvinists."

"Their father Satan gives them wisdom. Take care, captain, that you are not carried away by their doctrines. The true faith will triumph, depend on that," said the priest, frowning as he spoke.

"Your arguments are conclusive. It will not be

my fault if the plan miscarries," answered Villegagnon. "I will keep on the mask till I feel myself strong enough to throw it off."

"You will do well. Do not be in a hurry. We must get as many of these pestiferous sectarians into the net as possible."

Further conversation of the same character was held between the two worthies for some time. Nigel had found himself most unintentionally acting the part of an eavesdropper. He had at first felt inclined to start up and make the captain and priest aware of his presence; but as the conversation went on he felt that he was justified in thus learning the character of the leader of the expedition, whose evil intentions he hoped he might be the means of counteracting. He determined, therefore, to appear to be fast asleep should they, on quitting the room, discover him.

As he saw them rise, he closed his eyes. He heard their footsteps as they approached the door. Just then the light which Villegagnon carried fell upon him.

"I had no idea that any one was in the room," whispered the captain, holding the lamp towards Nigel.

"Who is he?" asked the priest, in a low voice.

"A young pig of a Scotchman, whom the admiral insisted on my taking on board as an officer."

"Should he have overheard what was said, he might interfere with our proceedings," observed the priest. "Your dagger would most speedily settle the question, and prevent mischief."

HE DETERMINED TO APPEAR TO BE FAST ASLEEP.

"I am not fond of killing sleeping men, holy father," answered the captain, in a somewhat indignant tone. "Even had the youth been awake, he is so little acquainted with French that he could not have understood what we were saying; but, you see, he is fast asleep. I, however, will keep an eye upon him, and shall soon learn whether he knows anything. If he does, we have frequently dark and stormy nights at sea, when men get knocked overboard. Such may be his fate; you understand me."

"A good idea. I will trust to your discretion," said the priest, and, greatly to Nigel's relief, they left the room.

He remained awake, considering how he should act. At length he heard some one enter the room; it was the captain, who, just taking a glance at him, threw himself on the bed, and was soon fast asleep.

At early dawn Nigel awoke, and, putting on his garments, went down into the yard to get some water to wash his hands and face. The rest of the party were soon on foot.

The captain met him in the morning with a smiling countenance, and, as he did not even allude to his having shared his room, Nigel thought it better to say nothing about the matter. He looked about for the priest, but he was nowhere to be found, nor did Nigel hear any one allude to him. It was evident that he had come and gone secretly.

The rest of the journey to Havre was performed without any other incident worthy of note. Three stout ships were found in the harbour, already in a forward state of equipment. Nigel went on board the *Madeline*, with several of his travelling companions, and at once took possession of the cabin intended for his use. The officers and the crew, as far as he could learn, were all Protestants, as were undoubtedly the passengers who had already come on board.

He found plenty of occupation in receiving and stowing the provisions and stores, and in setting up the rigging and bending sails. He was thus kept actively employed for several days, till the *Madeline*, the most advanced ship, was fully ready for sea. All the passengers, he observed, came off at night, to avoid the observation of their countrymen. Although the ships were already crowded with almost as many people as they could carry, there were still two vacant cabins on board the *Madeline*.

CHAPTER V.

UNDER WEIGH—ARRIVAL.

MORN had just broken; a southerly wind blew gently down the harbour, and Captain Villegagnon gave the order to lift the heavy anchors from their oozy beds.

"A boat is coming from the shore and pulling rapidly towards us," said Nigel to the captain. "The people on board her are making signals. Shall we stop weighing the anchor?"

"Yes, without doubt," answered the commander, looking towards the boat. "I thought that they had abandoned their design. We are still to have the advantage of the count's assistance and company."

Nigel looked eagerly towards the approaching boat. Besides the rowers, there were several passengers, two of whom he saw were females, and at length, as they approached, he recognized the Count de Tourville. His heart began to beat more violently than it was wont to do. He felt almost sure that the lady by the count's side was his daughter Constance. All doubt in a few minutes was set at rest, when the count, leading his daughter, came up the broad ladder which had been lowered to allow them to ascend. Constance gave him a smile of recognition as he bowed low, as did the other officers standing round, to welcome her and her father on board.

The squadron was now quickly under weigh, and gliding rapidly down the river. The weather looked fine, and all hoped for a prosperous voyage. Many who had narrowly escaped with their lives from the Romanists began to breathe more freely as the ships, under all sail, stood down the channel. Yet there were sad hearts on board, for they were leaving their beloved France a prey to civil strife, and their fellow religionists to the horrors of persecution, so that for the time they forgot their high hopes of founding another France in the New World.

As Nigel paced the deck in the performance of his duty, he was often able to stop and speak to the count and his daughter, and to render her those attentions which a lady so frequently requires on board ship. Often they stood together watching the distant shore or passing vessels, or the porpoises as they gambolled in the waves. Insensibly they became more and more drawn together. Constance told him of the difficulty she had experienced in escaping from the court. Had not her father himself, at a great risk, gone to Paris, she would have been unable to accomplish her object. Fortunately for her, a relative residing in the capital having fallen ill, had sent an earnest request to see her. She had been allowed to go, and had the same night left Paris with her father in disguise, travelling night and day in time to reach Havre just as the ship was on the point of sailing.

"We may hope now, however, to get far away from the follies of courts and the trickeries of politics to found a new home where, with none but true Protestants around us, we may enjoy the exercise of our religion undisturbed," she said, looking up at her companion with a smile.

"I trust that it may be so," said Nigel.

"What! have you any doubts on the subject?" she asked.

"I would not willingly throw a dark shade across the prospect you contemplate," he answered, "but we should be prepared for disappointment, and I believe few on board have thought sufficiently of the difficulties and dangers we shall have to encounter."

Nigel had expressed his thoughts more plainly than he had intended, and he regretted immediately afterwards having said so much. The conversation he had overheard at the inn frequently recurred to him, and considerably damped his ardour. To whom could he venture to communicate the knowledge he had obtained of the commander's character?

Who would, indeed, believe the young foreigner thus bringing so serious an accusation against the officer selected by Coligny himself, and of considerable renown as a naval chief? If he were not accused of malicious motives, the meeting would be looked upon as having only taken place in his dreams, for he should have to confess that he remained perfectly still during the time, with his eyes closed, as the captain and priest entered and quitted the room. He resolved, therefore, simply to keep a watch on Villegagnon, and to endeavour, if possible, to counteract his schemes.

Sometimes he thought of speaking to Count de Tourville, for he had, at all events, full confidence in his honour and discretion; but even he, knowing how much the admiral esteemed Villegagnon, might disbelieve him. He was compelled, therefore, to keep the knowledge he had obtained shut up in his own bosom. His chief satisfaction arose from the thought that Constance de Tourville was on board, and that it would be his joy and pride to defend her from all danger.

The weather, which had hitherto been fine, gave signs of changing. The wind shifted more to the west, and dark clouds came rolling up. The vessels, instead of gliding smoothly on, were now tossed about. The storm increased. The sails were reduced to the smallest proportions, but yet the stout ships could with difficulty battle with the waves.

Under other circumstances, the emigrants would have loudly petitioned to put back; but as it was, they were afraid, should they again set foot in France, of being seized by their persecutors; nevertheless, as the storm increased, the terror of the emigrants, unaccustomed to the sea, became greater and greater. Loud cries of alarm arose; some mourned their folly in having left their native shores to perish in the ocean. Nigel and the other officers did their utmost to calm their fears, and assured them that should the ships be in real danger they would return to the port.

Constance was among the few ladies who exhibited no undue alarm, and expressed their confidence in the skill of the officers. But even they at length acknowledged that they should be thankful could they find themselves again safe in port. The Count de Tourville especially was unwilling to return; but for his daughter's sake, however, he at length consented to ask the captain to do what he considered best for the safety of the ships.

"They will probably, if we continue at sea, become so battered, that we shall hardly reach our destination," was the answer.

The signal thereon was hoisted from the commander's ship, and the squadron stood back for France. On making the land, they found that they were to the eastward of the port from which they started, and at length they entered that of Dieppe. Here several of the artificers, and even some of the men of higher rank, resolved to abandon the expedition, rather than again risk the dangers of the sea. Their places, however, were supplied by others collected by the captain, who had gone on shore for the purpose. So many of these men were received on board each of the ships, that they became overcrowded; but the captain silenced all complaints by asserting that, if they would consent to suffer a little present inconvenience, they would have a greater number to defend themselves against any enemies they might meet with.

Once more the squadron sailed, and succeeded in getting clear of the Channel. They had not, however, been long at sea before Nigel began to suspect the character of the new comers, of which his own ship carried the greater number. They herded together, and showed little respect to the services which the chaplain was wont to hold on board for the spiritual benefit of the colonists. They were even seen to mock while he preached, till complaints, being made to the captain, he ordered them to behave themselves.

Day after day the ships sailed on, keeping close together, the wind being fair and moderate. Sometimes it fell a calm, when the officers and gentlemen Calvinists of the different ships visited one another, and discussed their plans for the future. The chief delight, however, of most on board was to hold religious services, which they could now do without fear of interruption; and hymns of praise arose from amid the desert ocean, their voices, when the ships were close to each other, uniting together in harmony.

Often had Constance expressed her feelings at the thought that they might in future thus worship God. Before, however, they reached their destination, they encountered several violent gales, during which, whenever his duty would allow him, Nigel made his way to the side of Constance to afford her comfort and support.

"Do not be afraid," he said; "our ships are strong, and our commander experienced. I have been in a worse found vessel in a more violent gale, and we reached port in safety."

"But the waves look so terrible, threatening every moment to come down and overwhelm us," said Constance, who was seated on deck, gazing at the tumultuous ocean.

"Remember, God tells us that it is He who rules the waves; and should it be His will, they cannot hurt us," answered Nigel.

"Yes, yes," said Constance; "I was wrong to express fear. Happy are we who possess the Bible, of which the followers of the tyrant Pope and his pretended priests are deprived."

"Think how many thousands of our countrymen would thankfully go through far greater dangers than we are enduring to reach a country where they may enjoy freedom from persecution," observed Nigel.

The young couple, however, talked on many other subjects; and when the storm ceased, and favourable breezes wafted them over the ocean, their spirits rose, and they spoke of the happy future in store for them. Nigel, however, was not altogether free from anxiety. He could not forget the conversation he had overheard between the captain and priest, though sometimes he almost fancied that it must have been a dream, Villegagnon was so courteous and polite to all his passengers, and expressed sentiments so in accordance with theirs.

At length "Land! land!" was shouted from the

mast-head. The goal of their hopes was near, and the ships, getting close together, glided with a fair breeze towards the magnificent Bay of Nitherohy. Lofty and fantastic mountains, then unnamed by Europeans, rose out of the blue waters before them. On the left, appeared the conical-shaped height, since known as the Sugar Loaf. Further on, on the same side, the Three Brothers reared their heads to the skies, and still more to the south was seen the Corcovada and Gavia, the green mountains of the Three Brothers strongly contrasting with the latter-named peaks, while the distant ranges of the Blue Mountains rose in the interior. On the right was seen another range of varied-shaped heights, extending far away to the north. Passing beneath the lofty Sugar Loaf, the flotilla sailed through the entrance, when the magnificent land-locked expanse opened out before them, surrounded on all sides by hills and lofty mountains; while lovely little verdant and palm-clad islands appeared dotting the dark bosom of the water. Words, indeed, fail to describe the beautiful and varied scenery. The anchors were dropped close to one of the first isles they reached. On this spot Villegagnon told the eager crowd who surrounded him that he had determined to form the first settlement of the new colony. Here, at the entrance of the harbour, and surrounded by water, they might defy the attacks of enemies from without, or the Portuguese or natives who might venture to dispute their possession of the country. From this they might extend to others on either side, and then form a settlement on the shore, thus advancing till they had brought under subjection the whole of the surrounding country.

The settlers expressed their satisfaction at the captain's plan, as they gazed at the richly coloured woods which covered the sides of the surrounding hills, at the purple blooming quaresma, the snake-like cacti, and the gorgeous flowering parasites hanging down even from the jagged and precipitous sides of the Sugar Loaf, and the rich verdure starting forth from every nook and crevice of the fantastically shaped rocks. Scarcely had the anchor been dropped, than the sun set behind the distant mountains, and, as darkness rapidly followed, they remained on board during the night.

Next morning, Constance and her father came on deck, where they found the young lieutenant attending to his duties. Again they gazed with renewed pleasure at the wild and the sublime outline of the surrounding mountains with their varied combinations, while the richness and beauty of colouring thrown over and around the whole, by the purple and rose colours and ethereal blue of the sky, imparted to the scene a beauty which no fancy sketch of fairyland could surpass. As they turned their eyes towards the nearest shore of the main land, they saw the beach and fringing rocks covered by a multitude of natives, waving green boughs as a sign of welcome; while, on the heights above, they had kindled numerous bonfires, to show their satisfaction at the arrival of the French, whom they believed had come to protect them from their enemies, the Portuguese. Preparations were being made on board the ships to land the officers and artisans, with materials for building the proposed fort. Villegagnon, in his barge of state, proceeded towards the shore to open negotiations with the native chiefs. He had requested the Count de Tourville to accompany him, and Constance begged that she might also go. As it was a mission of peace, no danger was apprehended; and it was thought that a lady being seen in the boat would give further assurance to the natives of the pacific intentions of their visit. Nigel, being one of the tallest and best-looking of the officers, was selected to steer the barge. Four other boats followed at a short distance. Their crews were fully armed, but were ordered to keep their weapons out of sight, and only to advance should the Indians show any sign of hostility.

As the barge neared the shore, a tall and dignified chief, his dress of the richest skins, and ornamented with gaily coloured feathers, with a circle of plumes on his head, holding an unstrung bow of great strength in his hand, was seen standing on the beach to receive the new-comers. By his side was a youth, strongly resembling him in features, bearing his shield and quiver, and also handsomely dressed, while other chiefs were drawn up in a semi-circle a short distance behind him, with the rest of his people collected on either side. He advanced a few paces with dignified steps, and, stretching forth his hand to offer a friendly grasp to the captain as he landed, announced himself as Tuscarora, chief of the Tamoyos.

According to Indian custom, he made a long harangue, welcoming the strangers to his country, and assuring them of his friendship.

"You come at a fortunate moment, when your aid may render us essential service in assisting us to defend ourselves against the assaults of a tribe of white men, who, for some years past, have attempted to establish themselves on our shores. They call us idolaters, and pretend to be of a religion which hates idolaters; but they themselves have numerous figures of men and women, before which they bow down and worship, and they fail not to shoot or cruelly ill-treat those of our people who fall into their hands; we, therefore, do not trust to their religion or promises."

The chief concluded by assuring the French that they were welcome to take possession of the island off which their ships lay, or of any other they might select in the bay. Villegagnon replied that he and his people came in the character of true friends to the Indians, and his great object was to obtain their friendship and support, and that their religion taught them to consider all worshippers of figures and pictures and any visible object as idolaters; their desire being to serve the great Spirit who watched over the Indians as well as over themselves, and that by their acts they would show that they were worthy of the confidence their new friends were evidently disposed to place in them. He expressed a hope, also, that by an exchange of commodities, and by mutual support, they would learn to regard each other as brothers.

During this address the Indians preserved the most perfect silence, though the eyes of the young chief, who stood by his father's side, wandered towards the boat in which the rest of the visitors still retained their seats. An attendant, now advancing, lighted the calumet of peace, which Tuscarora presented to the captain, who, after drawing a few whiffs, returned it to the chief, who performed the same ceremony. The rest of the party now landing, the pipe was passed round among them. Constance, who stood by her father's side, regarded the scene with much interest. She could not avoid remarking the glances of admiration which the young chief cast at her, and was compelled more than once to turn round and speak to Nigel, who remained close to her. He himself observed the looks of the young chief, which created an undefined feeling in his breast, though his pride forbade him in any way to exhibit it.

"These Indians are of a far more martial and gallant bearing than I had supposed; but still they are savages, and we should be wise if we are on our guard against them," he observed to Constance.

This was said aside, while Villegagnon was replying to the address delivered by the Tamoyo chief, who then introduced the handsome youth standing by his side as his son Tecumah, "who will ever, as he regards my injunctions, be a friend and ally of the French," he added.

The young man in a few words expressed his desire to act according to his father's wishes, winding up, as he pointed to the sky, "Should Tecumah fail to fulfil his promise, may the great Spirit punish him as he will deserve."

Thus far the interview had passed off in a most satisfactory manner. The chief expressed his desire to visit his new allies, but Villegagnon thought it prudent to decline the honour till the fort was erected, and the colonists were in a position to defend themselves, and at the same time to make such a show of their strength as might overawe the Indians, in whom they were not inclined to place more than a very limited amount of confidence. The Portuguese were at this time settled in a town which they called St. Vincente, about fifty miles to the south, the first colony founded by them under Martin Alfonso de Souza; and as there were many brave adventurers among them, Villegagnon thought it probable that as soon as they heard of his arrival, they would send an expedition against him.

The meeting with the chiefs having been brought to a conclusion, the boats returned to the ships, on board which every one was now engaged in landing stores for the construction of the proposed fort. As numerous trees grew on the island, they were cut down, and formed an abundance of material for the purpose. The artisans, who knew the importance of speed, laboured assiduously, and the work made rapid progress. The chief fort was built on the eastern side of the island, to resist the attack of a hostile fleet; and in the course of a few days the guns were mounted, and the colonists considered themselves fully prepared for defence. Houses were also commenced, and those weary of their long confinement on board ship hoped soon to take up their residence on shore. The natives brought over in their canoes an abundant supply of provisions, and, delighted with the beauty of the climate, the settlers felt thankful that their steps had been directed to so happy a spot, and looked forward with confidence to the time when they might see a handsome city rise on the shores of the bay. Now, too, they could all meet together to read God's Word, and to listen to the preaching of their minister without dread of interruption.

The chief of the Tamoyos, with his son Tecumah, attended by a number of the principal men of the tribe, arrived in a fleet of canoes to pay their promised visit to the white men. Villegagnon received them at the head of his seamen, and all the settlers drawn up under arms. The Indians were evidently much struck by the martial appearance of their new allies, and almost as much so by the progress which had been made in the settlement, as the fort, with its guns, and the houses, were already erected. It was a Sabbath morning, and at the usual hour a bell summoned the settlers to worship. Tuscarora seemed to fancy that some magical ceremony was going forward, and was afraid to enter; but Tecumah, less superstitious than his father, and prompted by curiosity, begged leave to attend, accompanied by several other young men. Though they were unable to comprehend a word, their countenances exhibited the most perfect seriousness and apparent interest in what was going forward. The count, who had observed

Tecumah, whose eyes, indeed, had seldom been turned away from the spot where he and his daughter sat, sent for the interpreter to inquire of the young chief what opinion he had formed.

"It is clear to me that you worship a great unknown Spirit, and that you sing to Him songs of praise, while your teachers exhort you to love and obey Him, and He is, I am sure, pleased with such worship. I remarked how it differs from that of the Portuguese, who make idols of painted wood, and bow before them as if such things could hear, or understand, or give help to the foolish men who put faith in such nonsense."

"And is such the opinion you have formed without having the principles of our faith explained to you?" asked the count, astonished at the intelligence displayed by the young chief.

"I have said what I conceive to be the truth," answered Tecumah. "I would like to know more of your faith, since it enables you to be as wise and powerful as I see you are. Some time since, during an interval of peace, I visited the settlement of the Portuguese. There I saw bearded men bowing down, some before a cross with a figure nailed on it, others before a woman with a child in her arms; others, again, were adoring an infant in a cradle; and others, men and women, in long robes, with books or staffs in their hands. Some were worshipping even pictures, and I thought that all these things were the gods of the Portuguese. When they told me that the woman with the child in her arms was the Holy

Virgin, and that the child was also a god, I could stop to hear no more, feeling sure that the great Spirit to whom the Indian looks up as God would be displeased with such blasphemy."

"Undoubtedly He is," said the count; "but had you inquired further, you would have been told that the figure on the cross and the child in the woman's arms and the one in the cradle represented the same person, the Saviour of mankind, who is now in heaven, at the right hand of God."

"Then, how can He be in heaven and on earth at the same time?" asked the Indian. "And if He is in heaven, surely men of sense should lift up their hearts to Him there, and not bow before figures which can have no resemblance to him; for I observed that even the infants differed from each other. And who, tell me, does the figures of the woman represent?"

"She was one especially honoured among women, but who the Saviour expressly showed He did not desire should be worshipped," answered the count. "She was chosen to be the earthly mother of the Son of God, who so loved the world, that He desired to become man, that He might be punished instead of all men; for all, being by nature sinful, deserve punishment, and God, who is all just and all merciful, decreed that all who believe that Jesus, His Son, was punished for our sins, should have those sins washed away, and be received into favour again by Him. Thus, Jesus came into the world as an infant, grew up to manhood, and, after setting an example to mankind by the obedient, pure, holy life He led, He allowed Himself to be put to the most cruel of deaths on the cross, such as the vilest of malefactors were alone considered deserving of. To prove that He was God, by His own will and power He rose again and ascended into heaven, there to be the Advocate and Mediator of those He had redeemed. Through Him alone the prayers of those who believe in Him can be offered and be received acceptably by God."

The young chief listened attentively to what the count said. "This is very wonderful, very wonderful," he observed, after being for some time lost in meditation. "I would wish to hear more about the matter; yet it strikes me as strange that God should allow His name to be profaned, and these senseless images to be worshipped instead of Himself."

"You are right, my friend," said the count. "God is a Spirit, and must be worshipped in spirit and in truth. He is also long-suffering and kind, and therefore He does not punish men as they deserve, that they may have an opportunity of turning from their sins and being reconciled to Him."

The count gladly took the opportunity of explaining further the truths of the Christian faith to the young chief, who seemed to drink in eagerly every word he heard. It was the first of many visits he paid, and often was his canoe to be seen, as the shades of evening drew on, skimming across the tranquil waters of the harbour towards the mainland.

The Indians received such entertainment on their first visit as the French could afford; and while it was yet daylight they returned in their canoes to the shore.

One evening the count and his daughter were sitting in their house with several guests, among whom Nigel was one. They had met to read God's Word and to sing the hymns of Marot, which the **French Protestants** loved so well. The weather, hitherto fine, had, before sunset, given signs of changing. Dark clouds were seen gathering eastward, and already a **damp and chilly** wind blew up the harbour's mouth, while the sea rolled in, sending its billows with an angry roar against the foundations of the new fort. As the tempest increased, **a gun** fired from each of the ships summoned their respective officers and men on board, and Nigel had unwillingly to hasten away from the house of his friend. It was not without difficulty that the boats reached the ships. The topmasts and topgallant masts were sent down on deck, and fresh anchors were got out. The settlers, as they saw the masts of the ships through the gloom, rolling from side to side, and watched the furious waves rushing in from the sea, began to tremble for their safety. They had, however, to think of themselves. The wind rapidly increased, the tall trees still remaining on the island bent before it, and the waves washed over the walls of the fort with relentless fury, threatening every moment to overwhelm them. Villegagnon, who had remained on shore, fearing that the guns might be lost, ordered them to be dragged out of the fort to a place of safety. It was a task of no slight danger, for already the woodwork trembled at each assault of the billows, and scarcely were the guns removed than, crash succeeding crash, large fragments of the fort, the construction of which had cost them so many days of labour, were rent away, and either carried off by the retiring seas, or thrown high up on the shore.

Constance de Tourville anxiously watched the progress of the storm. She had accompanied her father and several of their friends to watch the ships which lay in the harbour exposed to its fury. They could see the foaming waves dashing against them, and breaking high over their bows. Soon one was seen to be moving, when a single sail was set, and away she sped into the darkness up the harbour. The others dragged their anchors, or were torn from them, and were likewise compelled to seek for safety in some sheltered spot. With good pilots on board, this might easily have been done, but no one had a knowledge of the upper parts of the harbour, and it was impossible to say in what direction they might seek for safety.

That night was one of deep anxiety to all the settlers. The furious waves, surging round the little island, swept over the lower parts, and threatened at times to overwhelm it. Many of the trees, deprived of the support of their neighbours, which had been cut down, bent before the gale. Branches of some were torn away, others were broken off, and some uprooted from the ground. Several of the newly built houses were unroofed, and others were thrown down altogether by the wind. That of the count stood firm, and he and his daughter gladly offered shelter to as many of their friends as it could contain.

Constance, who had had a sleepless night, waiting till dawn broke, sallied forth to look for the ships.

Not one of them was in sight. In vain she made inquiries of those who had come, like herself, to look for them. No boats remained on shore; indeed, with the waters of the harbour tossing about as furiously as they were, even the largest could not have made her way amidst them. The Indians, from whom alone they could obtain any information, dared not venture across, and thus they must remain in ignorance of what had become of the ships till, the tempest being over, those which had ecaped destruction should return.

"Vain is the help of man. In God let us put our trust. He may think fit to preserve them; if not, we must say with confidence, 'His will be done,'" said the minister Laporte, addressing those assembled on the beach.

CHAPTER VI.

NIGEL'S RETURN TO FRANCE.

EANTIME the governor had been surveying the damages committed by the storm, and, summoning the count and other leading people, announced his intention of abandoning the island before more labour had been expended, and settling on another higher up the harbour. All approved of his proposal, for though they saw that the island was well placed for defence, it was also exposed to the fury of the sea when excited by tempests. They now awaited anxiously for news of the ships, but still the wind blew furiously up the harbour, and would prevent them from coming down, even should they have escaped shipwreck. Fears were entertained that they might have been cast on the northern shore, when their crews would most probably have fallen into the hands of the Portuguese. For two days more the tempest continued, and the hearts of the colonists remained agitated with doubts and fears. The third morning broke bright and clear, the clouds dispersed, and the wind, changing, blew with a gentle breath down the harbour. Had a boat remained on the island she would have been sent in search of the missing ships. Some proposed building a flat-bottomed raft, which might be finished in a few hours and serve to navigate the smooth waters of the bay. Villegagnon gave the order to commence the work, and already it had made some progress, when a shout was raised of "A sail! a sail!" It was one of the ships standing down before the wind from the upper part of the harbour. Another and another appeared, till at length the minds of the colonists were set at rest. They all had had narrow escapes, but had succeeded in bringing up under the lee of different islands, where, the water being smooth, they had ridden out the storm. Every one capable of labouring immediately set to work to reship the guns, and stores, and even the woodwork of the houses and forts, to convey them to an island Villegagnon had fixed on in a more secure part of the harbour. The task occupied several days, and sorely tried the patience of those who were anxious at once to commence their intended agricultural pursuits. The advantages possessed by the new spot selected were evidently superior to those of Lange Island which they had left. The count proposed that the name of their patron, "Admiral Coligny," should be given to their present resting-place, and he was supported by the leading colonists. The governor, with a bad grace, consented, though it was evident that he had intended to bestow his own name on their new acquisition.

With the exception of the losses caused by the storm, all hitherto seemed to be going on well; and Nigel began to hope that Villegagnon had abandoned his design, and really intended to establish a colony on the principles proposed by the admiral. He was glad, indeed, that he had not spoken of his suspicions to Constance or her father, as they must have been, had he done so, greatly troubled about the future. He, in common with all the officers and men of the expedition, was busily engaged from morn till night in erecting the new fortifications, which were laid out on a much larger scale, and were built far more substantially than the last had been. The colonists' dwellings were also re-erected, and, wood being abundant, many of them were of considerable size, though only one story in height. Within the fort were the barracks for the soldiers, while a number of houses to afford shelter to the inhabitants, should the settlement be attacked, were erected. The larger residences were scattered about over the island, and a village sprang up on the shores of the chief landing-place. It was, however, well protected by the fort, off which lay the ships, and it was considered that while they remained it would be secured against an attack. Four smaller forts were also built on commanding situations in the more accessible parts of the island, as Villegagnon considered that the settlement was well able to resist the assaults of either a civilized or barbarous foe. The friendly disposition shown by the Tamoyos, the most numerous and powerful tribe in the neighbourhood, gave him no anxiety on the latter account; while, although by this time the Portuguese settlement in the south had greatly increased, the Portuguese had shown no disposition to advance towards the shores of the bay of Nitherohy. It was the intention of the French to form a settlement on the southern shore of the bay as soon as their numbers were sufficiently increased; and Villegagnon, relying on his secure position, resolved at length to send back the fleet for reinforcements.

Nigel had in the mean time been a frequent visitor at the house of the Count de Tourville, where he ever received that friendly welcome which made him hope that he would not disapprove of his aspiring to the hand of Constance, who appeared to have no doubts on the subject. She knew that Nigel was of noble birth though destitute of fortune, and she felt sure that her father would not refuse to give her to one, her equal in birth, who was of her own religion, and whose heart was hers, while he was well able to protect her. They had not hitherto spoken of love, but they were mutually aware of the state of each other's affections, the most perfect confidence existing between them. Occasionally a holiday was allowed, when Nigel, having one of the ship's boats at his command, took the count and his daughter, with other friends, across the bay, to visit its picturesque shores and the many lovely islands

IN THE HEART OF THE FOREST

resting on its bosom. The party had gone higher up the bay than they had hitherto ventured to do, and reaching a small island which appeared to be uninhabited, they went on shore, proposing to dine and wander through its shady woods. The seamen remained near the boat, while Constance and two lady friends, with the officers and other gentlemen who formed the party, proceeded to a clear spot beneath the shade of some lofty trees, where for awhile they could enjoy the sea breeze, while discussing the viands they had brought. The repast being over, the three ladies strolled along the beach to the western end of the island, for the purpose of enjoying the view which extended almost to the extreme limit of the harbour. Constance's two friends had seated themselves on the bank, while she, attracted by some flowers which grew near the edge of the water ran forward to examine them. She was on the point of picking one of gorgeous hue when a canoe, paddled by a single Indian, unobserved by her, darted round the point and approached the beach. The occupant sprang lightly on shore, when a cry from her companions made her look up, and she saw a tall and handsome native, with a circlet of feathers on his head, and a cloak and kilt richly adorned, standing before her. Her first impulse was to fly, but, giving another glance at the stranger, she recognized Tecumah, the young chief of the Tamoyos. She had already acquired some knowledge of the language.

"What brings you here?" she asked. "We thought that none of your people were on the island."

She felt that it was better to speak, although she was not altogether free from fear. The respectful attitude of the young chief, however, reassured her.

"I often come here," he answered. "Seeing your boat approaching, I waited for an opportunity of speaking to you, lady. For days and days I have longed for it. Since my eyes first rested on your countenance it has never been absent from my heart. My ambition has been to become like your people, and to gain the knowledge they possess, and thus be worthy of leading you home as my bride."

Such in substance was what the young chief said, although his address was far longer, and more full of figurative expressions than have been here given. Constance at first could not understand what he said, but when its meaning broke on her she felt no small amount of alarm and uneasiness, yet her right feeling would not allow her to treat young Tecumah, savage though he was, either with contempt or anger.

"You have surprised and pained me," she answered gently. "It is not the custom of the maidens of my country to wed with those of another race or of a different faith," she answered. "I grieve to hurt your feelings but what you have asked can never be granted. Continue, as heretofore, to be the friend of my people, and you will also remain my friend. Let me now return to my companions, for they cannot fail to be surprised at seeing you; only let me ask that you will never repeat what you have just said, and banish me, I pray you, from your thoughts."

"Not while Tecumah breathes the air of heaven

can your form be banished from his heart. Oh, ask him not to perform a task beyond his power," answered the Indian. "He obeys you now, as you will find he is ever ready to do. Farewell." Saying this, greatly to the relief of Constance, the Indian with slow steps returned to his canoe, while she hastened back to her companions.

"Who is he? What object brought him here?" asked one of the young ladies in a tone of alarm.

"He certainly did not appear unfriendly," remarked the other. "I should say, Constance, judging from his manner, that he is a devoted admirer of you. Come, my dear, confess—did he not ask you to become his bride? Ah! I thought so," she continued, observing the colour rising on Constance's cheek.

"I cannot reply to you!" exclaimed Constance, feeling excessively annoyed at her friend's remarks. "You would not for a moment suppose that I should listen to such a proposal. I scarcely, indeed, could understand what he said. But we must not remain here, and it will be well if we return immediately to the boat, lest more of the savages should be lying concealed in the island and intrude themselves on us."

This last observation induced her companions eagerly to follow her advice, evidently more alarmed than she was, and as they hurried on they frequently looked back, expecting to see a party of dark-skinned warriors suddenly start forth from the forest near them. They, however, reached their friends in safety.

On finding themselves safe on board the boat they recovered their spirits, and the other ladies even ventured to banter Constance about her Indian admirer. Nigel naturally inquired what had happened. Constance then told him of the sudden appearance of the Indian, but the expression of her countenance prevented him from asking further questions. The expedition, which all agreed had been a very pleasant one, terminated without any further incident worthy of note.

Nigel, as usual, spent the evening at the count's house; and he and Constance found an opportunity before the other guests arrived, for strolling out in the woods behind the house, through which several walks had already been cut. She then frankly told him what had occurred, begging him, at the same time, not to be anxious on that account, as she had every reason to believe that the young chief would not again molest her.

"I trust not, dearest Constance!" exclaimed Nigel, taking her hand. "Would that I had a right to protect you. Will you consent to become mine if your father will give his permission?"

Constance gave him her hand. He spoke of his want of fortune, but he reminded her that he had a strong arm and willing heart, qualifications of no slight importance in a new colony, and he had every reason to hope that he should be able to maintain her. She agreed that he should immediately speak to the count, and he offered to throw up his commission and cast in his fortune with her father and his associates;

and before they returned to the house many a plan for the future was agreed on.

The count, almost to their surprise, without offering any objections, entered into all their views ; and Nigel determined the next morning to ask permission from the captain to quit his ship and settle on shore.

"Impossible, sir," was the answer. "Were I to give you the permission you ask all the officers and men would be desiring to turn settlers. I intend to send the ship back immediately, and you must be prepared to attend to your duty."

In vain Nigel expostulated ; Villegagnon threatened to put him in irons and send him back as a mutineer if he refused to obey his orders.

The ships were rapidly got ready for the voyage. Nigel, with a sad heart, bade farewell to Constance.

"Rest confident of my love," she whispered. "We must wait till you can obtain the admiral's sanction to quit the service. My father will write to him on the subject, and I doubt not that he will grant your request."

Still, though Constance spoke with confidence, the hearts of the young people were sad, for they could not help thinking of the many dangers which they both would have to encounter. Those to which Constance might be exposed rose up before Nigel. The settlement might be attacked by the Portuguese, or the natives might prove treacherous, and he could not forget his doubts of Villegagnon's honesty. Constance thought of the storms and the enemies Nigel might have to encounter during his voyage, and the risk he might run of being treated as a heretic by the Roman Catholics on returning to France. With forebodings she could not overcome, she saw the ship's sails spread to the wind as they glided out of the harbour.

The voyage to Europe was accomplished without any disaster. While the ships were refitting, Nigel, accompanied by Monsieur Billard, captain of the *Vesta*, one of the ships of the squadron, made a journey to Rouen, where the admiral had come to meet a number of persons who proposed embarking. The advantages to be gained in the new colony had spread among the Protestants of France, and persons of all ranks and from all quarters were eager to embark. The undertaking was especially favoured by Calvin, Farel, and other Protestant ministers, who hoped ere long to see a large and flourishing community of their fellow-believers established in the New World, where many of those suffering in Europe might fly for refuge.

Rouen was a large and populated place in those days, and the new emigrants had no difficulty in finding accommodation. Nigel and Captain Billard called on the admiral at his hotel, and were received with great courtesy and kindness. Nigel presented the count's letter.

"I am sorry, my young friend, for one reason, that you desire to quit the navy of France, for I feel sure that you would have risen to distinction," observed the admiral, "although I may congratulate you on another account; and I, therefore, do not hesitate to grant your request. You will, I hope, succeed in the new position you have chosen."

Nigel thanked the admiral, and afterwards, accompanied by Captain Billard, went to call on several persons of distinction who were about to proceed with them to Nitherohy. He had particularly wished to go on to Tourville to see his old friend the steward, so as to be able to give to the count a report of the state of his property. So eager, however, were the emigrants to set out, that the ships were got ready with unusual rapidity, and he had no time to make the journey. He was walking in the evening through the streets, when he caught sight of a person in ecclesiastical dress, whose features he recognized, and on a second glance he felt sure that they were those of the very man he had seen in company with Villegagnon. He suspected that the priest was there for no good purpose. The Jesuit regarded him with his keen grey eyes, and evidently recognized him, and when Nigel and his companion passed on, followed them at a distance.

The next morning, accompanied by a number of emigrants, they set out for Havre. Most of the party were men who followed civil occupations; the gentlemen, however, carrying swords, while a few among them had pistols.

On reaching Honfleur they found a large crowd assembled in the market-place, through which they had to pass on their way to the boats, which were waiting to carry them on board their ships. In the crowd Nigel again caught sight of the priest, who was speaking to the people around him.

" Come, come, my friends," cried Captain Billard,

who rode at the head of the party; "we wish to reach the boats waiting for us."

"They are heretics, despisers of the Holy Virgin and the saints!" cried some one from the crowd. "Down with them. Cut them to pieces. Let none escape."

Scarcely were the words uttered than a shower of stones was hurled at the heads of the Protestant emigrants, who immediately drew their swords to defend themselves, while they forced their way through the crowd. Scarcely, however, had they got many yards before they were met by a body of men, some with firearms, and others with spears and axes.

"We must fight for our lives, my friends," cried Captain Billard. "On! on! But keep together."

The bold front which he and his companions showed for a time kept back their assailants; but a voice, which Nigel recognized as that of the priest, was heard shouting, "Down with them! down with them!" and the mob again pressed them close. Many were wounded, and Nigel, with grief, saw his friend fall from his horse, shot through the body. He in vain endeavoured to rescue him. The savages dragged him into their midst, hacking and hewing his inanimate form. Nigel, seeing that he and his friends would be cut to pieces, urged them to keep close together; and by desperate efforts they at length cut their way down to the boats, from which the seamen, who were fortunately armed, leapt on shore, and, furiously charging the mob, turned them back and kept them at bay while the emigrants embarked.

NIGEL'S RETURN TO FRANCE. 95

On counting their numbers, it was found that, beside the captain, three others had fallen, while many were wounded. Providentially the women and children, with their baggage, had been sent on the day before from Rouen, or the whole party would have been cut to pieces.

On reaching Havre, Nigel and two other officers went on shore to complain of the outrage, but could obtain no redress from the authorities, who merely shrugged their shoulders and declared they could not restrain the religious zeal of the people. The anchors were speedily got up, and with sad hearts the emigrants left their native shores.

A fair wind carried the squadron down Channel, and for some time the voyage was prosperous. Before, however, they reached the latitude of Madeira the weather changed, and a heavy gale coming on, sorely tried the imperfectly prepared ships. The officers, exerting themselves to the utmost, encouraged their men, and the pumps were kept going till the storm ceased and the leaks could be got at and stopped. When the ships, which had been scattered by the gale, again joined company, all were found to have been sorely battered. One had lost her topmasts, another her bowsprit, and the rest some two or more spars. They had no friendly port into which they could put, as Madeira was in the hands of the Portuguese, so they had to wait for a calm to repair their more serious damages. The Line was crossed without having the opportunity, and when within three or four days' sail of their destination, some strange ships were seen ahead, apparently waiting for them. There could be no doubt that the strangers were Portuguese. A consultation was held by the captains whether they should try to escape by altering their course, or stand boldly on and attack the enemy. Water and provisions were running short, and should they take to flight, days and even weeks might elapse before they could gain their port. They determined, therefore, to stand on, and should an attempt be made to stop them, to fight bravely as long as their ships should swim. Their enemies were not to be despised, they knew, for the Portuguese of those days were renowned for their hardihood and courage. Five sail were counted, the number of their own ships, so that each would have an antagonist to contend with.

The French, under all sail, keeping close together in line, stood towards the headmost of the enemy's ships, which were somewhat separated from each other. Nigel's being the leading ship of the French squadron, first came up with the headmost one of the enemy's ships. They were sailing, it must be understood, on two sides of an angle, the French before the wind, the Portuguese close hauled. Captain Beauport, the commander of the *Madeline*, immediately hauled his wind and poured in his broadside at close quarters, bringing the enemy's mizenmast, with its large mizen, down on deck. The effect was to make the ship pay off before the wind, and expose her stern to the fire of the *Madeline's* guns, which had been rapidly reloaded and run out. Captain Beauport then running up on the larboard side of the Portuguese, so as to place himself between her and the rest of the enemy, continued the fight broadside to broadside, while he threw out a signal to his consorts to attack the other ships of the enemy. They, though considerably larger than the French, after exchanging a few shots at a distance, put up their helms and ran off before the wind, leaving the first ship attacked by Captain Beauport to her fate. This was soon settled, for though her guns and crew greatly outnumbered those of the *Madeline,* so many of her people had been killed and wounded, that as the French ship ran alongside for the purpose of boarding the enemy, the crew of the latter hauled down their flag and cried for quarter. This was immediately given, and efforts were made to stop the shot-holes through which the water was running into the prize. There seemed very little prospect of keeping her afloat. Her crew and passengers were in despair, and were eager to take refuge on board their captor. Many of the men, instead of endeavouring to save the ship, fell down on their knees, invoking the Virgin and saints to assist them. Captain Beauport and his officers, however, soon stirred them up, and insisted on their going below and attending to their duty. Among the passengers were two priests, who seemed especially anxious to save some cases and packages, loudly calling on their countrymen to assist them.

"Never mind your baggage, my friends," said Nigel. "Let the men attend to their work. If your property is lost, patience. We must first save all the water and provisions, in case the ship should go down,

G

as it will be difficult enough to feed all your people from our own stores."

"But, Monsieur officer, our property is invaluable," cried the priests. "It cannot be replaced. You do not know what precious things we have got."

"Precious or not, they must stay where they are till the shot-holes are plugged, unless you choose to carry them yourselves."

"Oh, sacrilegious heretic, we will be revenged on you some day," muttered one of the priests, while the other hurled some curses at Nigel's head, to which he did not stop to listen, remembering the proverb that "Curses, like birds, go home to roost at night."

By plugging the shot-holes and setting strong gangs to work the pumps, the prize was kept afloat sufficiently long to get out some of the provisions and water, as well as a portion of her cargo. The priests again loudly called on their countrymen to assist them in transferring the goods to the *Madeline*, though few of them showed any disposition to do so, but by the assistance of the French crew, their valuables were at length got out of the sinking ship.

The rest of the fleet had now come up, and the prisoners were distributed among them. The priests, however, would not desert their baggage, which, they insisted, was their own private property.

"If it is found to be so on inspection you shall retain it," observed Captain Beauport; "but as the cases may possibly contain munitions of war, we cannot allow them without examination to fall into the hands of your countrymen."

The priests protested that there was nothing warlike in them, but the captain was determined to have the cases examined. On opening them one was found to contain a large coarsely painted figure of the Virgin and Child, another half a dozen small figure of saints, the third was full of flat leaden figures and crosses.

"What are these?" asked the captain, coming to a fourth, full of small boxes and parcels.

"Those," answered the priest, who was looking indignantly on, "are the bones of saints and martyrs. Let them not be touched, I beseech you, by sacrilegious hands."

Each package was labelled, a score or more having the name of St. Anthony.

"Why, you must have got two or three saints' bodies here," exclaimed the captain.

"Only a very small portion of one, indeed," answered the priest; "a hair from his beard or a paring from his toe-nail is of value equal to the whole of his leg."

"And what are these other packages?" inquired the captain.

"Each contains some precious relic, efficacious in curing every disease to which the human body is liable," answered the priest.

"Nonsense!" exclaimed the captain; "we cannot allow such rubbish to remain on board."

"You will be guilty of horrible sacrilege and unheard-of cruelty to the settlers and poor natives, if you throw these precious relics into the sea, and deprive them of the benefits they will bring."

"We will see about it," answered the captain. "What are these bales?" he asked, pointing to some canvas packages, which he ordered his men to rip open.

The priests made no reply. They were found to contain sheets of paper, printed some in Portuguese and some in Latin, but all sealed with the seals of the ecclesiastical courts in Portugal or at Rome. They were, indeed, "Indulgences," or "Pardons" for various sins mentioned in the Romish Rubric, the prices, which varied from half a dollar to seven dollars, being marked upon each, the latter being for murder and the most heinous offences of every possible kind, which cannot be mentioned.

"Why, I see none for heresy, or sacrilege, or calling the Pope and his cardinals gross impostors, and you two worthies are arrant rogues and fools, or we might have become purchasers to a large amount!" exclaimed the captain indignantly. "Heave this trumpery overboard, and you, Senhores priests, may be thankful that you have been deprived of the means of cheating your countrymen and deceiving the ignorant natives by your abominable impostures."

The sailors, with shouts of satisfaction, forthwith hove overboard the boxes of relics, the bales of "indulgences," and the leaden charms, which quickly sank to the bottom. Some cases of trumpery rosaries were found and dispatched the same way. The images, or rather the idols, for such the natives would have regarded them, were lowered overboard, and went bobbing about astern of the ship, and the water soon washing off the paint, reduced them to the appearance of shapeless logs. There were still several cases of crucifixes of all sizes, having the appearance of silver but were found to be of iron, covered with the thinnest tinsel. The priests pleaded hard to have them preserved.

"No," said Captain Beauport, firmly; "I will be no party to your impostures. These are images as well as the others, and more blasphemous still, seeing that they have in no way the appearance of the crucified Saviour; and He Himself has said, 'Thou shalt not make unto thee any graven image, or any likeness of anything that is in heaven above, or that is in the earth beneath, or that is in the water under the earth: Thou shalt not bow down thyself to them, nor serve them: for I the Lord thy God am a jealous God'—and that I am sure you would have taught the natives to do, for your own people do the same; and so, to prevent you or others from thus offending God, they must be put overboard with the rest of your idols."

The priests swore oaths deep, but not loud, that they would be revenged on the heretics—oaths which they fully intended to keep. Sail was now made, and the ships stood towards the land. They had not gone far, however, before the signal was made from the prize that the water was again rushing in. The *Madeline* and the other ships sent their boats to her assistance, but all the efforts of the crew could not keep her afloat, and they had barely time to escape from her, when she went down head foremost, with most of her cargo on board. As the French had no desire to retain their prisoners, they steered into a small port some way to the southward of Nitherohy. Here the Portuguese were put on shore, with a supply of provisions and such arms as were required to enable them to protect themselves against the natives, who, they averred, would otherwise attack and cut them off—an event, considering the cruelties they had already begun to practise on the unfortunate Indians, very likely to happen. A bright look-out was kept during the time for the enemy's squadron, but it did not appear; and the French, favoured by a fair wind, steered for Nitherohy, which they were all eager to reach. Nigel's heart beat with anxiety. Besides knowing that the Portuguese, in considerable force, were in the neighbourhood, and being uncertain as to the fidelity of the fickle Indians, he could not forget his suspicions regarding Villegagnon, and he dreaded to hear that the governor had carried out the treacherous designs which he believed him to entertain. All eyes were directed towards the island-fortress, as the ship sailed up the harbour. Great was the satisfaction of the voyagers as they beheld the flag of France blowing out above the fortifications. Cheers burst from their throats, and a salute fired from the shore was returned by the ships, as, gliding on, they came to an anchor before the landing-place.

CHAPTER VII.

TREACHERY.

VILLEGAGNON stood waiting on shore to receive the new comers, who landed amid the cheers of their countrymen. He expressed himself highly pleased with this accession of strength to the community, and loudly declared that he believed ere long their Protestant colony would be established on a firm basis. His letters, he said, informed him that many thousands of French settlers were about to sail and join them. Nigel hastened on shore as soon as his duties would allow, and was welcomed with all the marks of affection he could desire by Constance, and kindly greeted by her father. Great progress had been made, the count told him, and he hoped that they should soon be able to form a settlement on the mainland.

"But we have been so happy here, that I should be sorry to move," said Constance, pointing to a pretty garden seen from the window of their sitting-room. Think of all the pains we have bestowed on it, and, should it be deserted, in a few months, in this climate, it would again become a wilderness."

"We must keep it as our country residence, and come here occasionally from our house in the new city," observed the count; "or perhaps you and Nigel will like to make it your home."

"Oh, that will be delightful," exclaimed Constance, "though I suspect that Nigel will require a larger sphere of action than this little island would afford."

They talked much more about the future, which, to the eyes of Constance, looked bright and happy. The count, however, when alone with Nigel, expressed his anxiety on several accounts. The governor had of late shown especial favour to the men he had collected to supply the place of those who had abandoned the expedition; and they were engaged in erecting a building, which it was very evident was intended for a church. Why there should be any secrecy about the matter the count could not tell; but it was a suspicious circumstance, as chiefly those who had refused to attend at the Protestant service were engaged on it. Still the governor professed to be as warm a Protestant as ever.

"Have you any suspicions of the honesty of his intentions?" asked Nigel.

"From this circumstance, and others which may

seem trifling, suspicions have arisen in my mind," answered the count.

Nigel then told him the reason he himself had to doubt the governor's honesty.

"I wish that you had told me of this before," said the count. "I should probably have returned with you to Europe, rather than have supported such a man by remaining. However, your explanations satisfy me that you acted, as you thought, for the best. We must now endeavour to counteract his designs."

They agreed not to speak to Constance about their suspicions of the governor, as the matter would not fail to make her anxious.

Nigel had to return to his ship at night; but, early the next morning, he again went on shore to visit his friends, intending also to apply to the governor to be discharged from the naval service. As he was nearing the landing-place, he observed a canoe, urged on towards the shore with rapid strokes by an Indian who plied his paddle, now on one side, now on the other. In the stern sat another person, a young girl, whose dark tresses were ornamented with a wreath of natural flowers, which gave an additional charm to her beautiful features, the rest of her costume being also adorned with gaily-coloured feathers, further increasing the picturesqueness of her appearance. She lightly stepped out of the canoe, followed by her companion, who hauled it up on the beach at the same time that Nigel landed. They together made their way to the village as if well accustomed to traverse the path. Nigel was a few paces behind them, and observed that they entered the house of the minister, Monsieur Laporte. On reaching the count's house, he mentioned the circumstance to his friends, and inquired who the Indians were.

"They must be, without doubt, the young chief Tecumah and his sister Cora, who come frequently to receive from our good minister instruction in the truths of Christianity, of which, I trust, they have gained considerable knowledge," answered Constance. "First the young chief came by himself, and then he begged permission to bring his sister. She is a sweet young creature; a perfect child of nature; and has already become even a more faithful believer than her brother, who cannot, as yet, understand why he should not destroy his enemies wherever he can find them."

Constance had before told Nigel of her meeting with Tecumah; she now assured him that the young chief seemed to have got over any attachment he might have felt for her, so Nigel felt no sensations of jealousy. Nigel proceeded afterwards to call on the governor to present his letter from the admiral. Villegagnon received him in his usual courteous manner, and complimented him on his gallantry with the Portuguese. When, however, he read the letter, his manner changed.

"The admiral does not command here," he observed, "and I require officers on board my ships. I cannot accept your resignation."

TREACHERY. 107

Nigel expostulated in vain. Instead, however, of at once refusing to serve, he resolved to take time to consider the matter. He went back to consult the count, who advised him to do nothing rashly; as, should he throw up his commission and come to live on shore, he would offend the governor and put himself completely in his power.

While they were speaking, Tecumah and Cora, with Monsieur Laporte, came to the house, to pay their respects, they said, to the count and his daughter. Tecumah recognized Nigel, and spoke to him in a way which showed that he desired his friendship. While Constance was conversing with Cora in a mixture of their respective languages, each doing her utmost to make herself understood and understand what the other said, Nigel found that Tecumah had made considerable progress in his knowledge of French; also, which was of more consequence, he was well acquainted with the fundamental truths of Christianity. Had they, however, touched his heart? There was the question; his actions alone would show that. Nigel inquired about the state of the country. Tecumah assured him that his own tribe and those in alliance with them were sincerely attached to the French. "But others in the north, who have had emissaries from the Portuguese among them, are not to be trusted," he observed. The Portuguese themselves were also increasing rapidly in numbers, and their town of St. Vincente was already of some size.

"My people, however, will keep a vigilant watch

on their proceedings, and I will give you notice, should we gain any intelligence of an expedition being prepared. Should one come, with your ships and with the assistance of our tribe, you will, without doubt, be able to drive back your enemies," he added.

While the young people were speaking, the count drew Monsieur Laporte aside, and was earnestly discussing with him the state of affairs.

The minister looked grave. "We must trust to Him who overrules all things for His own wise purposes," he observed; "and should reverses overtake us, we must not lose confidence in His love and justice."

Nothing occurred for some time to interrupt the usual occupations of the colony. At length, one morning a signal from the fort announced that a fleet was in sight. The gunners were summoned to the batteries; all the men got under arms, and the ships prepared for battle; getting springs on their cables, so as to haul themselves into a position to defend the landing-place.

As the ships approached, they were, to the infinite satisfaction of those on shore, seen to have the French flag flying at their mast-heads. There were five large ships and two smaller ones. It was hoped that they were bringing reinforcements of sound Protestants who would establish their faith in the land, and contribute to the material progress of the colony. As they drew nearer, salutes were exchanged, and they came to an anchor close to the fleet. The voyagers when they landed were warmly received by their countrymen, who did their best to treat them hospitably. There were people of all ranks, and from all parts of France. Several who had come in one of the larger ships were known to the count, who received them into his house. They stated that the fleet consisted originally of but three ships; but, as they were on the point of sailing, they were joined by two others conveying persons of whom they had been able to obtain no certain information. Villegagnon received all in his usual courteous way, but it was observed that he paid the most attention to those on board the latter ships. Before long it was whispered that among those people had been seen two men, who, though in secular dresses, were recognized as having been Romish priests. Still, though the people who had come in these two ships did not make their appearance at the Protestant place of worship to return thanks for their safe voyage, they were not seen to practise any of the rites of the Romish Church. Unpleasant rumours were, however, going about among the settlers, and the people asked one another how it was that the governor, who had professed to form a pure Protestant colony, should have allowed Romanists to come out among them. No satisfactory answer could be given to these questions, and some thought that the new comers were possibly lately converted from Rome, and would soon come to receive instruction from Monsieur Laporte. Others, however, shook their heads, and observed that, had they been new converts, they would have exhibited more zeal, and would have been the first to join hands with the older brethren; instead of that, they associated entirely with the suspicious characters who had all along shown a disrespect to the Protestant form of worship. All the settlers were, however, so busy in erecting dwellings, and cultivating the ground, that no one had time for polemical discussions.

Thus matters went on for some time till the church was finished. After it was roofed over, no persons, except those employed on it, were allowed to enter. Numerous cases, which had formed part of the cargo of one of the ships, were landed and conveyed to it, and a large bell was hoisted up into the tower. One Sunday morning the bell began to toll forth in a way which astonished the Protestant settlers. The church was thrown open, and those who had been suspected by their fellow-colonists were seen with triumphant looks wending their way towards it. Some of the Protestants, influenced by curiosity, went in, and, on their return, reported that they had seen the two priests clad in their sacerdotal dresses, standing before a richly adorned altar, with a crucifix over it, and the figure of the Virgin and Child, with those of several saints placed in chapels on either side. Mass, with all its accompaniments, was being performed, while the governor himself was taking part in the ceremony. The Count de Tourville, and several other leading Protestants, called on him afterwards to express their astonishment and regret at what had happened. He received them with a haughty air, and declared that it was his intention, for the good of the colony, to encourage both forms of worship equally.

The count expostulated. "The colony," he observed, "had been established for the express purpose of affording a home to Protestants, where they could, regarding religious matters, avoid those dissensions which had sprung up in the old country."

"You may still worship as you think fit; but others, who discover that they have erred in quitting the Catholic Church, have a right to enjoy the form which suits them best. I, as governor of this colony, am bound to please all parties, and I desire to hear no more complaints on the subject," he answered.

The deputation, being thus dismissed, retired to consult what steps should be taken. Though the Protestants still outnumbered the Romanists, the whole of the former could not be relied on, while the latter formed a compact body, most of them being thoroughly drilled by the priests, who had done their utmost to excite their fanaticism, while it was evident that they were supported by the governor. The Protestants, therefore, arrived at the conclusion, as people often do under similar circumstances, that nothing could be done, and that they must wait the course of events. The two priests appeared to be quiet, well-disposed men; they made no outward show, but were observed to be going about quietly, from house to house, especially among the soldiers; and every Sunday saw an increase in their congregation.

The count watched these proceedings with feelings of dismay. Monsieur Laporte exerted himself among his congregation, and urged them to study their Bibles, and to seek to live lives consistent with their

Christian profession. Many listened to him and followed his advice; but there were not a few careless ones who went over to join the party of the governor and the priests. The women were induced to go to the church to listen to an organ which had been brought out from France, while one of the priests, who was a good musician, instructed them in the art of singing. Fresh saints were set up, and additional ornaments were introduced, and on festal occasions the whole church was wreathed with flowers, imitating the custom of the heathens at their feasts of "Flora," and other festivals. These attracted the careless and giddy among the young, who found the idolatrous system, which their fathers had repudiated, well suited to their tastes. Thus rapidly the traitor Villegagnon and his priests won over the larger part of the population. In vain the elder people, who had seen the effects of Romanism in the old country, warned them and protested against the fearful errors which were being introduced. Many of the young girls and youths were induced to go to confession and receive absolution for their past sins; the result being that they sinned and sinned again with their eyes open, under the belief that they could be again absolved. Morality, which had been strictly maintained among the settlers, fast disappeared. The priests now openly sold indulgences, and went from house to house abusing those who refused to purchase them, and warned them that they would be considered as Protestants and heretics. The count and other Protestant elders, met and discussed what was to be done, but they had to confess themselves powerless. The minister preached more earnestly, and some few were won back to the truth; but the popular party still increased daily. The governor, it was observed, promoted only professed Romanists, and managed by degrees to dismiss the Protestant officers.

Villegagnon at length threw off the thin mask he had hitherto worn, and declared that the majority being in favour of Rome, the settlement must become what he called a Catholic colony. The Protestants complained loudly of the governor's treachery; and several of them were arrested on charge of mutiny, and for plotting against the established authorities. Captain Beauport coming on shore one day, as he was on the point of returning to his boat, was seized and carried off to a prison Villegagnon had lately erected in the fortress. He was not informed of the crime of which he was accused, nor could he conceive what it was, as he had carefully abstained from making any remarks on the conduct of his chief. The following day he was brought into the public hall of the fort, where the governor was seated as judge, supported by several of the officers whom he had promoted. One of the crew of the *Madeline*, with the two priests, appeared as his accusers, and his officers and several of his men were ordered on shore as witnesses, Nigel being among them. When the priests were called on to make their statements, one of them charged the brave captain with the crime of sacrilege, which, as it had been brought to his notice, he said that he felt bound to make it public. A seaman, then stepping forward, stated that by his orders, a number of holy images, crucifixes, and sacred relics captured from the Portuguese, intended for the conversion of the heathen and the comfort of believers, had been sacrilegiously thrown overboard on their voyage to Nitherohy.

"Of what immense value they would have been to us in the conversion of the heathen had they been preserved!" exclaimed one of the priests. "They were undoubtedly offered to us by Heaven, to enable us to convert the barbarous natives."

Nigel and the other officers were then called on for their evidence. They had to confess that they saw the articles mentioned thrown overboard; but Nigel observed, as they were part of the cargo of the prize, he could not suppose that the captain in any way acted contrary to what he was fully justified in doing.

"Beware, lest you are made a party to his crime!" exclaimed one of the priests. "I know well the malignant and impious disposition of your countrymen, and, had you not been imbued by their sentiments, you would have endeavoured to prevent so sacrilegious an act from being committed."

The governor, as judge, declared that no further evidence was necessary. In vain the captain asserted that he had acted as he believed right. The priests shouted out that he deserved to die, and the traitor, Villegagnon, forthwith pronouncing him guilty, condemned him to death.

Nigel, on quitting the court, hastened to the

SEIZURE OF CAPTAIN BEAUPORT.   (*See page* 113.)

residence of the count, to tell him of the result of the trial.

"This must not be," he said, on hearing it. "It would be a most atrocious murder. Every Protestant in the settlement must unite, and insist on having his life spared. It would be useless to petition; we must *demand* our rights."

Nigel fully agreed with the count, and other leading Protestants coming in were of the same opinion.

"We must stake our lives on the issue," exclaimed one of the boldest.

The count observed, that as it was their lives and liberties were in jeopardy, and that a bold front could alone save them. On separating they went among their friends to stir them up to action. That night every true Protestant capable of bearing arms assembled, and the next morning marched together to the fort. On their way they met a Roman Catholic, who thought that Captain Beauport had been unjustly condemned, and willingly undertook to convey to the governor the resolution to which they had arrived. They waited, advantageously posted for defence on the brow of a hill a short distance outside the fort, while their envoy went forward with their message to the governor. They had also sent messages on board the ships, the officers and crews of most of which were sound Protestants, and would, they had every reason to believe, support them in their endeavour to rescue the brave officer, who was loved and honoured by all, especially by his own crew. While waiting the return of their envoy, a messenger arrived from the fleet conveying the promise of the officers and men to afford them their full support. This made them still more determined to remain firm to their purpose. Their envoy soon afterwards returned with the reply of the governor, stating that he would take their demands into consideration. On hearing this, they desired him to go back again, insisting that whether right or wrong, with regard to the act, it was committed on the high seas, beyond the jurisdiction of the governor, and that, if guilty, Captain Beauport must be sent to France to be tried. The governor, finding so strong a force opposed to him, saw that he had been premature in showing his colours, and that it would be his wisest course to try and conciliate those whom he could not for the present crush. He accordingly, accompanied by several officers, went out to meet the Protestants. In the blandest style he could assume he assured them that he wished to act fairly towards both parties. He therefore stated his readiness to send Captain Beauport home for trial, and inquired whether any of the colonists who were dissatisfied with his government would wish to return to their native land. The idea had not before been entertained by them. Several, however, at once replied that they were willing to return home, and others said that they would take the matter into consideration.

"Captain Beauport, then, will be kept in safe custody, till the ships are ready to sail," said the governor. "They will be prepared in a few days;

TREACHERY. 119

and, before that time, I wish to be informed of the number who desire to embark."

The Protestants, on receiving this announcement, returned to their homes. These were mostly situated together, and, as they had now ample proofs of the treachery of the governor, they stationed men on the look-out to give notice, should he send a force to attack them, that they might immediately reassemble and defend themselves. A meeting was held to discuss their future prospects. A considerable number of the most influential people resolved to return to France, hoping to live there in obscurity, or to make their way to Geneva. Some, among whom was the count, resolved to go to England, should he find France in the same unsettled state as he left it. Nigel was now thankful that he had not abandoned the naval service, as he hoped that the *Madeline* would be sent home, and that he might again have the happiness of having Constance and her father on board. Still, the prospects of all the party were gloomy enough: many of them had embarked all their fortunes in the undertaking, and they would return without the means of support to their native shores.

On the following day, a considerable number of the colonists sent in their names as desirous of returning, when they were informed, to their dismay, that the three smallest ships only would be got ready to receive them. Reports had before been spread that so weatherbeaten and unseaworthy were these ships, that they were not again to be sent to Europe, but to be retained in the harbour for the protection of the colony. Nigel was almost in despair at receiving this information. He urged the count rather to remain than to run the risk of the voyage. The count, influenced by his daughter, was greatly disposed to follow the advice of Nigel, who observed that the *Madeline* would probably before long be sent home, and that he might then take a passage on board her. The whole community were in a state of alarm; and it was increased when the governor sent directing them to be prepared to embark on the following day, with the information that only two of the ships could be got ready.

That night the greater number of them met in their place of worship, to offer up their prayers to God, that He would protect them from the dangers they might have to encounter during their intended voyage. The meeting was almost concluded; Monsieur Laporte, in a loving address, was exhorting them to hold fast to the Gospel, whatever persecutions they might have to endure, when a loud knocking was heard at the door of the chapel. On its being opened, an Indian appeared in full war costume, with one of those formidable bows in his hand, with which the Tamayas boasted they could send a shaft through the mail-clad body of a foe and fix him to a tree.

"I am Tecumah!" he exclaimed. "Many here know me as a faithful friend of the French. I come to give you warning that a large force of your enemies and ours are on their way down the harbour to attack the island. They consist of Portuguese and their

Indian allies the Tuparas, who have transported their boats and canoes overland from the place where they have been secretly built for the purpose. They come in expectation of taking you by surprise, when, should they gain the victory, not a human being they may discover will be left alive. They have sworn to exterminate you and us by all the false saints they have taught their Indian friends to worship."

Some doubted the information brought by Tecumah; but the count and Monsieur Laporte urged their countrymen to believe him, as they well knew the warm affection with which he regarded them, and were convinced that he would not have alarmed them needlessly. Some time was thus lost, but at length it was agreed that the count, with two other of the principal persons, should at once haste with Tecumah to carry the information to the governor, and urge him to take steps for the protection of the settlement. Unhappily, the Protestant officers having all been removed from their posts, there was no one of authority in the congregation to send a direct order on board the ships to prepare for action. The night was unusually dark; not a breath of wind rippled the surface of the mighty estuary; and the ships, which were at anchor close together off the usual landing-place near the fort, could not move to any other position, where they might assist in the defence of the island, three sides of which were thus left unprotected. The enemy would certainly make their attack where they would not be exposed to the fire of the ships or that of the fort.

CHAPTER VIII.

ATTACKED BY ENEMIES.

ECUMAH urged the count and his friends to make all haste. Even now he feared that there would be barely time for the French to assemble and prevent the enemy from landing. Once on shore both parties would be on equal terms, and the most numerous would probably gain the victory. He had despatched a messenger, however, he said, to his father, to come with his warriors to the assistance of their friends, as, unfortunately, they were at a distance from their usual dwelling-place, engaged in hunting, and might not be able quickly to collect. The count had sent word to **Nigel** to warn him and the other officers of the squadron to be prepared for an attack, and also to entreat as many as could be spared to come on shore to be in readiness for the defence of the island. The Protestants had also got under arms, so that they might be able to march in any direction where their presence might be required.

The governor received the count and his companions in the haughty and insolent manner he had of late assumed, and at first appeared inclined to discredit the account Tecumah had brought; but when the young Indian, with all the eloquence of his race, assured him of the truth of his statement, and warned him of the danger of delay, he changed his tone. He was too sagacious an officer not to see in reality that the warning must not be despised, but, without deigning to thank the count and his companions for the information they had brought, he desired them to go back to their friends. They obeyed his orders; while Tecumah, having fulfilled his mission, hurried away to his canoe, intending to cross to the mainland for the purpose of urging his tribe to use all speed in coming to the assistance of the French. The governor, meantime, ordered the troops to get under arms, and sent off a despatch to the ships, directing the captains, some to get under weigh and to sail round to the other side of the island, others to remain ready for an attack near the landing-place. The calm, however, prevented the first part of his order from being obeyed.

The whole population of the island was speedily aroused, and began to assemble at a central spot appointed by the governor. Scouts were also sent out along the shore, and every precaution was taken which the sagacity of an experienced officer like Villegagnon could suggest. The women and children, whose houses were in the more exposed situations, were brought to the fort, though it was hoped that the enemy might be driven back before they could effect a landing. Scarcely, however, had the armed men collected, than the sound of firing was heard coming from the end of the island, where a little bay was situated. It was a spot which afforded an easy landing place; but a fort had been built upon it, which it was supposed was of sufficient strength to drive back any enemy who might approach it. Several shots followed the first, and then came through the calm night air the sounds of strife, the victorious warwhoops of the Indians, and the shrieks and cries of the conquered.

"Forward, my men, and drive back the enemy," exclaimed Villegagnon. "The fort has, I fear, been surprised, and the garrison cut to pieces, and, if so, the enemy have landed, and we must be prepared to encounter them on shore."

Saying this, the governor, who was not destitute of courage, led forward the main body of his men, while he despatched a messenger to the ships with an order for the seamen to advance to his support. The count with a small number of his men was ordered to keep in the rear, to act as he might think necessary. The darkness of the night prevented the French from seeing their invaders. They had not got far when they found themselves in the face of a force which

ATTACKED BY ENEMIES.

they could only estimate by the hot fire which was opened on them. They fired in return with equal vigour, but it was soon evident that they were greatly outnumbered. Several of them fell. Showers of bullets whistled amidst them, while flights of arrows came flying into their ranks. In vain the governor endeavoured to repel the foe. At last he gave the order to sound the retreat, intending to fall back on the fort. The unseen enemy pressed him hard, and their fire increased rather than diminished, showing that more had landed. The count had now led his men up to take part in the fight, but they could do no more than check the advance of the enemy, and prevent them from overpowering the party under the governor. Even the bravest began to despair of success. The flashes of the guns lighted up the darkness of the night, and where the fire was the hottest there the governor and Count de Tourville threw themselves fearlessly, exposing their own lives to encourage their followers. It was very evident that they had not only Indians, but civilized Europeans to fight against. Notwithstanding their bravery, they were quickly driven back; and, before long, the count saw that his own and the surrounding houses would be exposed to destruction. At length a shout was heard on one side. It was recognized as coming from the body of seamen who were advancing to their support. The governor immediately despatched an officer to lead them to a position he wished them to occupy; but, before they had reached it, they found themselves engaged with a strong party of the enemy who had been sent to intercept them. The fight was now raging in two quarters, but still the enemy appeared to be gaining ground.

Constance de Tourville had remained at home unwilling to desert the house till compelled to do so. Several other ladies, whose houses were in more exposed situations, had come there for shelter, and stood listening with anxious hearts to the hot strife going forward within a short distance. At length some of the party proposed that they should fly to the fort; though, dreading the governor, they were unwilling, if it could be avoided, to place themselves in his power. Constance preferred remaining, her father having promised to send timely notice to her should the French find themselves compelled to retreat. The sounds of the battle came nearer and nearer. Several of the ladies declared that they could remain no longer, and hurried to the door to make their escape; Constance remained firm.

"I will obey my father," she said; "and when he sends me word that it is time to fly, I will go."

The other ladies, influenced by her example, hesitated, when a shower of bullets came whistling above their heads, and shouts and shrieks and cries of the combatants sounded as if they were close at hand. It was too evident that such was the case. Constance herself began to await anxiously for the order from her father to quit the house; when suddenly, in addition to the other sounds, a chorus of wild warwhoops burst on their ears. The savage cries were replied to by the shouts and cheers of the

ATTACKED BY ENEMIES.

French. The musketry rattled as loud as ever, but none of the shots came near them. In truth, the Tamoyos had arrived just at the moment the governor had determined to retreat and take shelter in the fort, leaving the rest of the island to the mercy of the invaders. Tecumah was at the head of his tribe, who fought with the most desperate fury against their hereditary enemies the Tuparas. The Portuguese were now in their turn compelled to retreat; the French and Indians pressed them hard, and, finding their expectation of surprising the settlement defeated, they took to flight towards the bay where they had left their boats. Nigel had landed with a naval force, and, feeling that he was fighting for everything he held dear, he was regardless of his own safety. Again and again he led his men on against greatly superior numbers of the enemy, but till the arrival of Tecumah and his party all his efforts had been in vain. Again he was leading them on, when he felt himself struck by a bullet, and, staggering a few paces, fell to the ground. Still he called on his men to advance. The Portuguese and Tuparas every now and then faced about in order to cover the embarkation of those who first reached the boats. Their bravery secured the retreat of their friends, but the greater portion of the rear-guard were overtaken and cut to pieces, while the main body shoved off from the shore and made their escape.

Constance and her friends had been anxiously awaiting the issue of the strife. When they heard the sounds of battle receding, their courage rose, and they hoped that their countrymen were gaining the victory. Still they were left for a long interval. At length Constance determined to go out and ascertain what had taken place. They provided themselves with lanterns, several of which had been brought to the house by those who had taken refuge in it, and, aided by their light, they went courageously forward. They had a higher motive also. They knew too well that many must have fallen, and they hoped to carry succour to some of the wounded, who might have been left behind by their advancing comrades. After going some way, they reached a spot where the strife had been hottest. Here lay friends and foes mingled together, Frenchman and Portuguese; the Indians only being distinguished by their war-paint and fantastic costume. On all the bullet, or arrow, or the deadly hatchet, had done its work. As they cast their lanterns on the forms stretched on the ground they saw that their help could not avail. The wounded had either been carried off by their companions, or had dragged themselves away to seek assistance. Still they persevered in their mission of mercy, searching for others who might be still breathing. They were attracted by the sound of a groan, which proceeded from a spot not far off. Again all was silent.

"Here is a wounded man!" exclaimed one of the ladies, calling to Constance. "He is a naval officer, I see, by his dress."

Constance and her other friends hurried to the spot, and, by the light of a lantern cast on the countenance of the officer, Constance saw at a glance that he was Nigel. She threw herself on the ground, and endeavoured, with the help of her companions, to staunch the blood flowing from a wound in his side. He was pale as death, but another groan escaping from his lips showed her that he still breathed. At length they succeeded in stopping the effusion of blood. She called on his name, but he was too weak to answer, though once she felt, as she took his hand, a slight pressure returned, which showed that he recognized her voice.

"Oh, Marie, hasten to the house, and entreat some of our friends to come and assist in carrying him there!" she exclaimed to one of her companions. "Bring a bed, or a door torn from its hinges, on which he can be placed. We must not allow him to remain here longer than is possible. Quick, my dear, if you love me!"

Her friend hurried away, eager to bring assistance which the young officer so greatly needed. Constance in the mean time sat by the side of Nigel, resting his head on her arm, while she bent over him, and assured herself that he still breathed. Though dreading every moment to hear his last sigh, with loving and gentle words she endeavoured to recall him to consciousness. How fearfully long the time seemed. The sounds of the strife still going forward reached her ears, though she scarcely heeded them, for all her thoughts and all her feelings were centred on Nigel. Anxiously she and her friend waited the arrival of the party from the house. The latter every now and then got up and advanced a few paces to listen. At length lights were seen in the distance, and footsteps were heard approaching. Constance uttered an exclamation of thankfulness when she saw her friends approaching with a litter they had hastily constructed with three poles supporting a mattress. With gentle care Nigel was placed upon it, and the ladies lifting it from the ground proceeded towards the house. Soon after they had reached it, the count arrived with the intelligence that the enemy had been driven off the island, and that the boats of the squadron had gone in pursuit of them. His sorrow at hearing of Nigel's dangerous state was very great, and, ordering restoratives to be given him, he immediately set off in search of the surgeon, who had come out with the first party of the settlers, and had remained faithful to the truth. He happily discovered him attending to some of the wounded men who had been carried to one of the neighbouring houses. As soon as he could leave them he hastened to Nigel's side. After examining his wound, he expressed a hope that, by constant watchfulness and care, he would recover, though the loss of blood had greatly exhausted him, and all would depend on his being kept perfectly quiet. One thing was certain, that he would be unable to move for many weeks to come, without risking his life. On hearing the surgeon's report, Constance entreated her father not to carry out his intention of proceeding to Europe.

"I will certainly on no account leave him," he answered. "Possibly the ships may be delayed, or

CONSTANCE SAW AT A GLANCE THAT HE WAS NIGEL.

(See page 159.)

ATTACKED BY ENEMIES. 133

the governor will be unwilling to let them sail, on the probability of the island being again attacked; but if so, he must treat the Protestants with more justice than he has been doing for some time, and we must live in hopes that fresh arrivals from Europe will again turn the scale in our favour."

Whether or not the governor suspected that the Protestants hoped, with increased numbers, to recover their influence, it was difficult to say.

The next day was devoted to rejoicings for the victory. The bells of the Romish church rang out, the fort fired salutes, and a procession with crucifixes, banners, and images, marched through the island. The priests sang praises in honour of the Virgin Mary, whom they asserted had given them the victory, in answer to their petitions. The Protestants assembled in their place of worship to return thanks to God for their deliverance. While the service, which had taken place at an earlier hour than usual, was going forward, an officer and party of soldiers arrived in front of the chapel. Without knocking, or asking for admission, the officer entered the chapel with his hat on his head, and, in a loud voice, exclaimed—

"I bring you an order from the governor to disperse. He will allow of no meetings, except in the church he has built for the use of the colony."

"Allow us, sir, to finish the service in which we are engaged," answered the minister, in a deep tone. "It may be the last many of us will enjoy for some time to come."

"My orders are to put a stop to your meeting,"

said the officer. "If you refuse to obey, I must use force to compel you."

Several of the persons present showed an inclination to dispute the point, but the minister and count urged them to yield obedience to the orders of the governor, and they quickly departed, when the officer, closing the door, put a seal on it, cautioning the people not again to enter, the governor having threatened severely to punish any who might do so. With sad hearts they returned to their homes. The victory over their enemies, instead of having improved their condition, appeared to have made it still more unbearable. Many who had before intended to remain on the island now determined to proceed in the ships which the governor announced would sail in a couple of days. When, however, they went on board to arrange their sleeping places they found the vessels in so battered and unseaworthy a condition, and so overrun with vermin, that many resolved to remain rather than undergo the risk of a voyage on board them. The officers and crews confessed that they were very unwilling to sail; at the same time, as they were all Protestants, they were anxious to get away from the island. The governor had also threatened them with punishment should they refuse. They promised, for their own sakes, as well as for that of their passengers, to repair the ships as much as time would allow. Indeed, the crews were already working hard to fit them for sea. If the governor would permit them to remain another week, they might, it was hoped, be placed in a tolerably efficient state to cross the Atlantic. The governor, however, would only allow them two more days, at the end of which time he insisted that all who intended to go must embark. A third of the original number, therefore, abandoned their purpose and resolved to remain and endure all the indignities to which they were likely to be subjected, while the rest, with many forebodings, went on board the two ships. They were, as it was, much overcrowded, and it was with difficulty that they could obtain sufficient provisions for the voyage, the governor asserting that no more could be spared from the stores of the garrison.

When all were on board, and the anchors were about to be weighed, Captain Beauport was led out from prison in chains under a strong guard, and, not being allowed to communicate with any of his friends on shore, was conveyed on board; the captain to whose charge he was committed being directed by the governor to deliver up his prisoner to the authorities at the first port at which he could touch, charged with rebellion and heresy. Captain Dupré merely replied that he would do his duty, as far as he had the power. He was a silent undemonstrative man, not given unnecessarily to express his opinions. He had never shown a disposition to disregard the orders of the governor, who was, therefore, persuaded that he would carry them out on the present occasion. With sad hearts those remaining saw their countrymen sail away. They were anxious about their fate; but they had still greater cause to be anxious about their own.

In the mean time, Nigel, under Constance's unremitting care, and that of the good surgeon who remained, was progressing favourably. Some days passed before he had sufficient strength to speak, and not till more than a week had elapsed would the surgeon allow him to be told what had happened; he was then deeply grieved to hear that the count and Constance had remained behind for his sake. He dreaded even more than they did the treachery and cruelty of Villegagnon, knowing him as he did to be so completely under the influence of the priests.

"He is but a wretched tool in their hands; and they, acting according to the dictates of their accursed system, which they call 'The Church,' are determined to drive every Protestant out of the island, so that they may again be masters over the consciences of all the inhabitants. Why," exclaimed poor Nigel to Constance, "did I not denounce the traitor to the admiral, who would not then, I feel convinced, have trusted the colony to his government? Even had I failed to convince him, it would have been better to have been dismissed, and to have sought my fortune elsewhere. But then, Constance, I should not have met you; and even now, if God wills that I should recover, I may be the means of preserving you from the dangers by which you are surrounded."

"You acted as you believed right, and you must not blame yourself," said Constance. "We must trust in God, and remember that, whatever happens, He orders all things for the best. Should He permit these wicked men to triumph, let us feel sure that He has some object in view, though we may not see it."

The count also exonerated Nigel from any blame, and was much inclined to find fault with himself for having quitted France, instead of remaining at his post, and looking after his dependants.

"We are but weak fallible creatures at best," he observed. "We often fancy that we are following God's will when we are pursuing only the promptings of our own inclinations. It shows how absolutely necessary it is to seek for guidance at the throne of grace in all our actions, even in what we may consider the most minute. When we remember that the hairs of our head are all numbered, and that God has told us that not a sparrow falls to the ground but He knows of it, we should remember that no act is too minute and inconsiderable to seek for counsel from Him regarding it. I might say that at every word we utter we should ask Him to direct us, for a single word may have an effect for good or for evil on those who hear it."

Still Nigel was not satisfied with himself. Few people can be so, when they review their past actions, unless they have acted as the count advised, and sought for guidance from above.

For a short time the Protestant settlers were left to act as they thought fit; but their place of worship continued shut up, and they were not allowed to enter it. They met, however, at each other's houses to read the Scriptures and offer up prayer and praise together. But they thought it wise to do so with closed doors, and they always had some one on the watch outside to give notice of the approach of any of the Papists. Indeed, they found it necessary to use the same precautions which they had been accustomed to employ in France. They were now subjected to the same persecuting spirit as that from which they had attempted to escape. Their only hope of being freed from their present galling condition was by a large influx of Protestant settlers, when the scales might be again turned in their favour. Would Villegagnon, however, allow such to land? In all probability he would send them over to settle on the southern shore.

This state of affairs continued for some weeks, during which Nigel slowly recovered, much owing to the loving care of Constance, and the skill of their friend, the surgeon. At length his health was considered fairly re-established. The count, however, advised him not to return to his ship until absolutely compelled to do so; indeed, having the permission of the admiral to quit the service, Villegagnon could not legally insist on his remaining in it.

"Indeed, my dear friend," said the count, "I feel that my own life is so uncertain, and should I be taken away, my daughter would be left without a protector in whom I could place confidence, that I desire forthwith to commit her to your care. You will, I know, devote yourself to her, and, as far as a human being has power, defend her from all dangers."

Nigel grasped the count's hand, and with a proud joy at his heart, promised not to disappoint his expectations. He took no vain oath: he did not call on God to witness that he intended to fulfil his promise, for he and the count knew that what he uttered was heard in heaven, and required no other ratification. Constance willingly agreed to her father's wishes, and it was settled that in a few days the marriage ceremony should be performed by their minister and friend, Monsieur Laporte. Their love was mutual and equally intense, and they felt that they could together face the dangers of many sorts surrounding them far better than apart. Constance implicitly confided in Nigel, and he felt unspeakable pride and joy in having the power of supporting and protecting her.

CHAPTER IX.

PROCEEDINGS OF "THE INQUISITION."

TEN days had passed since Nigel and Constance were united. He had not ventured beyond the precincts of the garden; and it might have been supposed that Captain Villegagnon had forgotten his existence, as no order had been sent him to join his ship. He intended, should he receive one again, to plead the admiral's permission to quit the service, Coligny having indeed accepted his resignation. As long, however, as he was not interfered with he resolved to remain quiet. He employed his time in assisting the count in the cultivation of the ground, and in devising plans for the future. Rumours were abroad that the governor intended on the arrival of fresh colonists to found a town on the north side of the harbour, to be named Nitherohy. The count determined to move there, and to purchase a plot of land on which to build a residence and form an estate, as he hoped before that time to receive remittances from his steward.

"I should not have thought of it, my dear Nigel, had it not been for you and Constance," he observed. "Though as regards myself all worldly pride and ambition have been laid aside, I should like to see you the master of a property suitable to your birth and education."

The idea was naturally consonant with Nigel's wishes, and he promised to labour hard in bringing the proposed estate into cultivation.

"It will afford me ample employment for the future," he observed; "and employment, of course, I must have."

Tecumah and Cora had during this time made frequent visits to the island. Tecumah was welcomed by the governor, as he was always well informed of the movements of the Portuguese and hostile Indians, besides having already rendered important services to the colony. The governor only looked on him in the light of an intelligent young savage and a faithful ally to the French. He had, however, already advanced in a knowledge of Christian truth, and had become an earnest and believing follower of the Lord. He one day came over to report that a party of the Tuparas had been seen on the high ground beyond the southern extremity of the harbour, making their way to the Portuguese settlement. He advised that boats should be sent out and advanced posts stationed, to give due notice of an attack, should one be contemplated. These arrangements having been made, the governor invited Tecumah to accompany him in a walk to a part of the island which he was about to visit. The strains of solemn music reached their ears. Tecumah attentively listened with much delight, and inquired whence they proceeded.

"The ministers of our religion are performing a sacred service, my friend," answered the governor. "If you please, we will enter and pay our devotions to the Holy Virgin and saints."

"I thought that Christians worship God alone," observed the Indian.

"Of course, so we do," said the governor; "but we worship also, in a different way, the mother of God and His holy saints and apostles."

"I have heard that God is a jealous God, and will have none other gods worshipped but Himself," said the Indian.

"But the mother of God; surely He will have us worship her?" observed the governor.

"The Bible does not say so," answered Tecumah, boldly. "When Jesus hung on the cross He said to John, 'Behold thy mother,' and to His mother, 'Behold thy son;' and looking round on His disciples,

He once observed, when He was told that His mother and brethren were near, 'Behold My mother, and My brethren.'"

"Where did you learn all that?" asked the governor, in an angry tone.

"From one of your good ministers; and I am sure he spoke the truth," answered Tecumah, innocently.

"He shall suffer for it," muttered the governor.

They had just then reached the door of the church, and Tecumah followed the governor, who went up towards the so-called "holy altar." The Indian gazed around with astonishment at the gorgeous drapery, the images, the lighted candles, and the large silver crucifix, with the figure of the Virgin on one side, and St. John on the other, and the vases of flowers, and numerous other ornaments. He said not a word during the whole ceremony, but watched attentively what took place. There was the usual chanting in Latin, and so-called prayers muttered over in the same language; while the church was filled with incense from censers waved to and fro. Then, during a solemn silence, the chief officiating priest lifted up something (what it was he could not make out) above his head. He then observed that they put something into their mouths and drank wine, which they had mixed with water from a silver cup. Then the people came up and the priests put something into their mouths, and there was more chanting and prayers in an unknown tongue. Then those who had been on their knees rose and filed out of the church, laughing and talking and making jokes with each other. Tecumah followed the governor, anxious to know what had taken place, and inquired what the priests were about when they muttered prayers over the silver dish and wine.

"They were then performing the greatest miracle of our Church," answered the governor. "They were converting the wafer and wine into the body and blood of Christ."

"What?" asked the Indian. "Christ has assumed His glorified body, and is now in heaven at the right hand of God. Which body, may I ask, do they think they eat, His human body or His glorified body? I cannot understand the matter."

"Nor can I enlighten you," answered the governor, looking much perplexed. "I am not fond of having such questions put to me."

"Pardon me if I ask one more," said the Indian, who was eager to gain information on the subject. "What were they doing when they lifted the wafer above their heads?"

"They were then offering up to God the great sacrifice, the real body and blood of His dear Son."

"Christ was once offered up as a sacrifice for sinners on the cross," said the Indian; "surely they cannot offer Him again?"

"Our Church says they can; and that's all we know about the matter," answered the governor, in a tone of irritation.

"Let me then ask you another question," said

Tecumah. "What were they doing when they ate the wafers and drank the wine, and then put the wafers into the mouths of the people?"

"They were eating the real body and drinking the blood of Christ," answered the governor, "and feeding the people with the body, for the priests alone are allowed to drink the blood. They were, in other words, performing the sacrifice of the mass."

"What?" exclaimed the Indian, starting back. "It is too solemn a thing to joke about; but do you wish to make me believe that the people can really believe that they eat the body of their God, and that human beings can change pieces of paste into that body? No, no, no! Monsieur Governor. We Indians have not a knowledge of the numerous arts you Frenchmen possess, but we are not so foolish as to believe such a gross imposture as that. I am afraid that your priests are like our medicine-men, in whom we trusted till we found them to be rogues and deceivers."

These words were uttered by Tecumah in a loud, indignant tone, and were overheard by one of the priests, who, having changed his gorgeous robes, had followed the governor out of the church in order to speak to him.

"Beware, young man, what you say!" he exclaimed, in an angry tone. "How can you understand the mysteries of our faith? But I know well where you received your instruction, and he who taught you shall have his just reward."

Tecumah stood calmly listening to the priest's

angry threats. "He who taught me is under the protection of my tribe," he answered, "and those who injure him will be our foes. I now see that you are one of the men who played the tricks in the church hard by, and deceived the people by persuading them that you have the power which belongs to God alone, to work a miracle."

These words so enraged the priest, that he would have struck the Indian had he dared. The governor observed his anger, and being well aware of the importance of not offending their Indian allies, on whose support their very existence depended, now interfered and tried to soothe the angry priest as well as Tecumah. The latter, however, felt more scorn than anger towards the man whom he, with his acute and unprejudiced mind, looked upon as guilty of practising a gross imposture, and he was therefore quickly pacified; but the priest, grinding his teeth, continued to mutter threats of vengeance, till the governor, drawing him aside, reminded him of the importance of not offending the Indians.

"You may do what you like with the heretic minister," he observed; "but the services of these Indians are required, and we cannot afford to lose them."

"The guilty one shall feel the vengeance of our Church, then," answered the priest. "We cannot allow a doctrine which so greatly supports our authority to be called in question."

"Of course not, my friend, of course not," said the governor; "though, as men of sense, you and

I no more believe in it than does that clever young Indian."

"As to that, Monsieur Governor, we keep our opinions to ourselves," said the priest, with as near an approach to a laugh as he ever indulged in. "At the same time, the sooner we put that acute, clever-minded young Indian out of the way, together with his instructor, Monsieur Laporte, the better for the maintenance of our holy religion." The countenance of the priest had assumed its usual undemonstrative expression as he continued, "Listen, Monsieur Governor. I believe that the Count de Tourville and his daughter and son-in-law are equally dangerous. That young Indian and his sister are constantly at their house, and have imbibed their pestiferous notions from them. I have had my eye on them for some time, when they were not aware that they were watched. I do my duty in looking after the spiritual interests of my countrymen"—the priest crossed his arms and cast his eyes on the ground—"but I feel that my humble efforts unaided are not sufficient. When our community increases, we shall have many of these accursed Protestants among us, and it will be absolutely necessary to devise effectual means for the preservation of our authority. I would therefore suggest the establishment of the Holy Inquisition, by which alone heresy can be rooted out. It will prove our zeal for religion, and gain the approbation of our patrons, the excellent Duke de Guise and his brother, the Cardinal of Lorraine."

"You will have my permission to carry out your

plan as you may wish, holy father," said the governor. "You may exercise your authority on our countrymen as you may deem necessary to bring them under the wholesome control of the Church; but I cannot have the Indians interfered with until we are strong enough to do without them. When we are, you will have my full permission to manage them as you think best for the purpose of bringing them into the true fold; but in the mean time their savage relatives may not understand your object in burning them for the good of their souls, and may be apt in their ignorance to revenge their deaths by cutting us to pieces."

"I understand your wise policy," answered the priest. "We will bide our time, then, for commencing the conversion of the Indians. But I have your permission to act towards the count and his family, and that pestiferous heretic minister, as I may judge necessary for the full establishment of the faith in our colony?"

"Certainly, certainly," answered the governor; "I willingly grant you all the power you ask."

The priest returned into the church to hear the confessions of several of his congregation, who were waiting to get absolution that they might sin again without having too great a load on their shoulders; as also to put out the candles, which he in his hurry had left burning. The governor returned to the fort, while Tecumah went to pay his usual visit to Monsieur Laporte. He naturally expressed his astonishment at what he had seen and heard.

"Surely," he exclaimed, "sensible men do not

really believe that, by the words of a priest, Jesus Christ, sitting at the right hand of God, really does allow His body to descend into the bits of paste which the priest puts into the mouths of the people. The Bible, as you read it to me, says that He is seated at the right hand of God, to make intercession for us sinners, and that He acts as our great High Priest."

"I cannot tell what the poor ignorant people may really believe, though it does seem astounding that they should be so imposed on by their priests," answered Monsieur Laporte. "It was many centuries even before the corrupted Church of Rome introduced the dogma or notion, which was invented by a monk in the eighth century, when it was eagerly seized upon by the Pope, who saw that it would enable him and his army of subordinates to become sacrificing priests, which would give them immense influence over the minds of people, if they could persuade them to believe it. They had taught the great mass of the people to believe in the power of dead men's bones and other relics to work miracles; in the heathen notion of purgatory for cleansing the soul by fire; to worship idols with the names of saints; to pray for the dead; and to pray to dead men whom they had dubbed saints, as well as to put faith in many other abominable falsehoods. They found, therefore, no difficulty in persuading the more ignorant people to believe this most blasphemous fable, which from henceforth became one of the most powerful engines for increasing the influence of the priests over the minds of men, though many, both learned and unlearned persons in our own and other countries loudly protested against the novel doctrine, as contrary to the true meaning of our Lord's language at the last supper and the teaching and practice of the apostles."

"I thought that you and other sensible men could not possibly believe so outrageous a notion, and so contrary to God's word," observed Tecumah. "But how comes it that men can be so wicked as to teach what is in direct opposition to the Bible?"

"Influenced by Satan, they make use of every means, however impious, to gain an influence over their fellow-creatures. It has been the same everywhere from the earliest ages of the world. They are like your medicine-men, whom you now know to be gross impostors. In all countries there have been found men, for their own ends, or for the support of the authority they serve, willing to deceive their fellow men, in many instances, as is often the case with these priests of Rome, being deceived themselves. Our only sure guide and prevention against such impostures is the study of God's Word and constant obedience to its holy precepts. As Jesus withstood the temptations of Satan by replying to him with the Scriptures, so must we arm ourselves, and ever be ready to withstand our foes, in whatever form they come, by the same blessed word of God. A sure sign that the Romish system is the invention of Satan is that it dreads the Word, and whenever it has the power, keeps it from the people or grossly misinterprets its meaning."

"I would that I could have that blessed Book

translated into the language of my people," exclaimed Tecumah. "I can now understand it in French, and may be able to explain it to those who are willing to hear me; but I should desire to send it throughout the whole country, that all the native tribes might hear the glad tidings that there is a loving Saviour ready to receive them into the kingdom."

The above conversation occupied a much longer time than we have in repeating it, and both the minister and young chief used very different language to that which has been employed. Tecumah showed by his questions and replies how completely he understood it, and how his pure unprejudiced mind revolted against the falsehoods of Rome, while it quickly embraced the truth of the Gospel.

After quitting Monsieur Laporte, he paid a visit to the count. He found Nigel hard at work in the garden, and Constance helping him. He repeated to them what he had seen and the impression formed on his mind, and they explained the truth much as the minister had done; to which Constance added an account of the horrible system of the confessional, which she had heard from some of her Papist friends, who had been subjected to it, and the abominable questions which had been put to them by the priests.

"That alone would have been sufficient to convince me that this system is not of God. And He tells us from the mouth of the Apostle Paul that we may come boldly to the throne of grace, trusting in the all cleansing blood of Jesus; and Jesus Himself says, 'Come unto Me, all ye that labour and are heavy laden, and I will give you rest.' I am sure that He never refuses to hear when a human being comes trusting to His blood shed on Calvary. Monsieur Laporte was reading from the Epistle of Timothy a prophecy that there should come 'some who shall depart from the faith, giving heed to seducing spirits, and doctrines of devils; speaking lies in hypocrisy; having their conscience seared with a hot iron; forbidding to marry, and commanding to abstain from meats, which God hath created to be received with thanksgiving of them which believe and know the truth,' who would advocate will-worship and their own good deeds in opposition to the all perfect atonement of Jesus. Such truly is what the priests of Rome teach, though nearly for a thousand years after Christ came Christian ministers, whom they acknowledged as belonging to their communion, were allowed to marry like other men; and certainly those who did so were less corrupt than the celibates who, having no family ties, became the servile tools of Rome's tyranny."

Constance had now to go in to prepare for dinner, and Nigel then asked Tecumah what remarks he had made to the governor and the priest. The Indian told him.

"You spoke truly; but knowing what these priests are, I fear much that they will endeavour to entrap you; and if they find that they cannot compel you to believe in their false doctrines and to acknowledge their authority, they will use other means to bring about your destruction."

PROCEEDINGS OF "THE INQUISITION." 153

"I will be watchful, and keep out of their power," said Tecumah. "I fear much, though, that they will equally endeavour to persecute you whom they look upon as my instructor; but I will be on the watch, and try to defend you as well as myself."

Tecumah spent the rest of the day with his friends, and it was late in the evening when his canoe was seen gliding rapidly across the harbour towards the mainland.

Villegagnon and the priests did not long allow the Protestant settlers to remain in quiet. The governor announced that he had received orders from France to allow no Bibles to remain in the hands of any of the people, declaring that they made a bad use of them by seeking an excuse from their pages for rebellion. The count resolved to go in person to the governor, and reminding him that he had ever been loyal, to claim exemption from the tyrannical law. He went, but was haughtily told that rich and poor must be treated alike, and that no exception would be made in his favour. Should he not deliver up all the Bibles in his house, he must be prepared for the consequences. Monsieur Laporte and the good surgeon were treated in the same manner. Nigel, however, resolved, as he was not a Frenchman, not to part with his Bible; and, in case a domiciliary visit should be paid by the "inquisitors," having placed it in a box and buried it in the garden among some thick trees, he and Constance could thus take it out and read it, which they did every day, without risk, as they supposed, of being discovered. Before long a party of men appeared, headed by an officer, with an authority from the governor to collect all the Bibles and Protestant sermons and hymns to be found. The count, knowing that resistance was vain, delivered up those he possessed, protesting, however, against the injustice of the act.

"That's not our affair, Count de Tourville," answered the officer; "but I will report what you say to the governor. Now, let me ask you, have you any other books?"

"I have given you all that are to my knowledge in the house," answered the count. "If you are not satisfied you must search for them."

"We cannot take the word of an heretic," said the officer, insolently. "We intend to search, and if we find any it will be the worse for you."

Providentially, Nigel was away, and thus escaped having questions asked him. Poor Constance endeavoured to console her father while the officers were searching in every corner and cranny of the house. No books, however, were discovered; and at length, threatening to pay another visit shortly, the inquisitors went away to search other houses in the neighbourhood; and in two or three, meeting with opposition, they carried the owners off to prison. The most severe sufferer was Monsieur Laporte, the whole of whose library was carried off, all his books more or less being of a theological character.

The following day, in an open space in front of the fort, a pile of faggots was seen, when the books were brought forth from the house into which they had

THE BONFIRE OF BIBLES.

been thrown. Most of the population turned out to witness the expected sight, shouting and jeering as book after book was thrown on the pile, to which fire had been set. As each fresh batch of books began to burn they shouted loudly, and when it was seen that most of the books were Bibles, their shouts and cries and fierce execrations grew louder and louder. This went on till all were consumed. The Protestants remained at home during the period, sorrowful and cast down. No one knew what persecutions they might be doomed to bear. Monsieur Laporte went from house to house, endeavouring to console and support his flock, reminding them all of the sufferings Christ's people had been called on to bear from the earliest days to the present time, and urging them to keep in view that crown of glory which He had prepared for all who hold fast to the truth. So much had his faithful and gentle character won the love of all except the most brutal, that many even among those who had been perverted regarded him with affection, while the priests, hearing him so highly spoken of, were afraid for the present to persecute him further. They were, however, very active among his congregation, whom they endeavoured by soft words and plausible arguments to win over; but finding that they did not succeed, as in reality only the frivolous and irreligious had hitherto been gained to their side, they determined to use harsher measures.

One evening Nigel and Constance had gone to their bower in the woods, where, concealed by the thickness of the surrounding foliage, they took out their Bible and sat down on a bench Nigel had placed there. He had been reading for some time to his young wife, occasionally stopping to explain a verse or to ask her opinion; now turning back and comparing text with text, both of them being so absorbed that they did not know how long they had been thus engaged, when they were suddenly aroused by hearing a footstep, and looking up they saw a priest standing before them, while a little way off appeared a party of armed men.

"You have been discovered engaged in an unlawful act, Monsieur Nigel, by which you have made yourself liable to the just vengeance of the law!" exclaimed the priest, in a triumphant tone. "You have been suspected for some time. In the name of the governor, therefore, I order you to yield yourself prisoner. Take this gentleman into custody," he added, turning to the armed men, who, as he spoke, sprang eagerly forward.

Nigel was too much astonished for the moment to reply. Constance uttered a cry of alarm, and clung to his arm.

"You cannot, you must not take him from me!" she exclaimed, in a terrified tone.

"You are equally guilty, young lady, in listening to him," said the priest. "In all probability you will share his fate."

"Oh, let me go with him now, then, if you insist on taking him," she said, still holding Nigel's arm.

"No, no, lady. Don't fancy that you will be allowed to keep him company," said the priest, in a harsher tone. "For the present you may remain with your father, till the governor thinks fit to summon you."

"Fly rather to the faithful Indians," whispered Nigel; "do not put yourself in the traitor's power."

He could say no more, for the armed men seizing him took him off, while the priest held Constance in his arms. She in vain struggled to free herself from his loathsome grasp, while she entreated to be set free, ever and anon uttering shrieks for help; but not till the priest was sure that the party with Nigel were out of sight did he allow her to escape, when seeing her father, who had been attracted by her cries, coming from the house, she flew towards him, the priest in the mean time hurrying after his companions. It was fortunate for him that he got away, for the count, with a thick stick in his hand, forgetting the danger of doing so, would have made him feel the effects of his just anger.

"Oh, save him, save him! They have seized Nigel. What will they do to him?" cried Constance, as she sank into her father's arms.

The count saw that pursuit was hopeless, for the priest, tucking up his long dress to enable him to scramble over the fences, had already got to a considerable distance; besides, it would have been vain to attempt rescuing Nigel from a party of armed men. The count could only say, "Trust in God, my child. He alone can help us."

Poor Constance, overcome with grief and terror, could scarcely, even with her father's assistance, reach the house. He placed her on a couch by his side, vainly endeavouring to console her. He indeed feared that the priests would not allow them to escape with impunity, and he guessed truly that it had been only for the sake of inflicting a greater cruelty that Nigel had first been carried off.

Monsieur Laporte with the good doctor happily came in, having heard a rumour of what had occurred. Both were required, for Constance became seriously ill; but the words of the former were of more value than any medicine the latter could prescribe. The minister at once turned to God's word; not to the Book itself, for that he did not dare to carry about, but to the numerous blessed texts which he had committed to memory, and from these he was able to draw that effectual comfort which could alone avail with the poor young wife. No one dared to speak of the future, for they knew well the bitter hatred felt by the governor and priests towards Nigel, and that they would rejoice at having a victim in their power on whom they would wreak their vengeance. While they were seated with Constance and the count, Tecumah and his sister arrived, on their way to pay their usual visit to Monsieur Laporte. They were overwhelmed with grief and indignation when they heard what had occurred. Cora threw herself by the side of Constance, and poured out her expressions of sympathy from her woman's heart. Indian as she was, she could feel for her white sister, her affectionate tones tending somewhat to soothe her friend's outraged feelings.

"Do not give up hope," she whispered. "We

will gladly devote our lives, if necessary, to save him. We Indians are accustomed to do many things which would astonish the white people, and if a friend is in danger, every one of our tribe is ready to help him."

"They dare not kill him!" exclaimed Tecumah, "and if a hair of his head is injured I will arouse our people, and instead of being friends and ready to fight on their side, we will come over with our strong bows and attack them."

"Even for the sake of a friend we would not urge you to use violent measures," said the minister. "Remember the precepts of our blessed Lord and Master; He who was ever mild, gentle, and forgiving, doing good to those who injured Him."

"Yes, I know that, and desire to obey our Saviour's law; but He does not forbid us to help our friends," exclaimed the young Indian.

CHAPTER X.

IMPRISONMENT AND RESCUE.

TECUMAH and his sister remained for some time with their friend. Tecumah then accompanied the minister to his house. They passed on their way through the count's garden, as it afforded them a shorter cut than the public path. As they got to the further end of the garden they turned aside to visit the spot where Nigel had been seized. On reaching it, Tecumah sprang forward, for there he saw before him on the ground the Bible, which the priest, in his eagerness to hold back Constance, had let drop, and had forgotten to take with him when the count appeared.

"Blessed Book!" exclaimed Tecumah. "Let me

IMPRISONMENT AND RESCUE. 163

be its guardian. Your cruel persecutors shall not burn it while I have it in charge, and you may come over to read it, or when the search is over I will bring it back to you."

To this proposal Monsieur Laporte willingly agreed; and while the Indian, wrapping it up carefully, concealed it beneath his cloak, the minister closed the box in which it was wont to be put, and covered it over again with earth and leaves.

Cora begged that she might be allowed to continue with Constance till the following morning or longer. "We were not observed coming into the house," she said, "and it will not be known that I am here. I have my reasons for wishing to remain."

The count and Constance of course agreed to what Cora wished. Before her brother quitted the house she had a short and earnest conversation with him. Tecumah, having spent some time with the minister, hurried to his canoe and rapidly crossed to the north side of the harbour.

Meanwhile, Nigel was dragged along by his captors. He had been so completely surprised that it was impossible for him to escape; and finding this, he walked along without making any further resistance.

The priest soon overtook the party. In vain Nigel tried to learn from him what had become of Constance.

"It's not my duty to answer questions," he replied; "but I have some, notwithstanding, to ask you. How is it that, knowing the orders of the governor, you ventured to read that book from which you draw all your heresies?"

"I am not aware that I have drawn anything but truth through the teaching of the Holy Spirit," answered Nigel.

"That is the notion all you heretics hold!" exclaimed the priest. "It is the origin of your pestiferous principles."

"I was not prohibited from reading it in my own country, and I claim as a Scotchman the right to do so wherever I am," answered Nigel.

"No person of whatever country has the right to act contrary to the commands of the Catholic Church," answered the priest, furiously; "and that Church positively forbids laymen from reading the Bible, or putting their own interpretations on it, therefore to whatever nation you belong you are under its rule, and are equally guilty. But I waste words in arguing with a heretic. Your only hope of escape from death is to recant without delay and become a faithful Catholic, and the governor, at my intercession, will overlook your offence. Come, you will be wise; so give up your errors."

"Never will I give up my faith," answered Nigel, firmly.

"Ah, my young friend, you say so now; but think of the advantages you will gain. You will at once be restored to your young wife, and will undoubtedly be raised to a post of honour and wealth in our new settlement; and when the count dies you will inherit

IMPRISONMENT AND RESCUE. 165

his property and found a noble family in Antarctic France."

Nigel felt that the temptations held out were powerful, but he prayed that were they ten times more so he might have grace to resist them. He doubted also very much whether the wily priest was not mocking him. He knew full well from the accounts he had heard in France of the treachery of which the emissaries of Rome were guilty, and he would not place any confidence in the most specious promises any of them might have made to him. He therefore let the priest talk on, endeavouring as far as he could not to listen to him. At length the fort was reached. Nigel was forthwith thrust into a cell, ordinarily used for the confinement of a refractory or drunken soldier, and was there left to his own meditations. He walked up and down, considering what he should do and what he should say. Now and again he stopped, and earnestly prayed for guidance and direction. The governor and priests were too eager to condemn the Protestants to allow an accused person to remain long in prison without trial.

That very afternoon Nigel was carried into the public hall where the governor held his court. The priest was his accuser, and the men by whom he was captured were the witnesses against him. Of course he had no defence to make, except his claim of right to read whatever books he pleased.

"Before he is condemned there is another charge of a still more heavy nature," said the governor. "Stand forward, men, and say what you have got to state;" and Nigel was, to his astonishment, charged with abetting Captain Beauport in heaving overboard the images of the saints, the relics, and papal dispensations.

"Even had I actually assisted I should only have been obeying the orders of my superior officer," said Nigel.

"You confess that you were guilty of standing by and witnessing such a proceeding without remonstrating?" exclaimed one of the priests who was seated near the governor. "Such enormities must meet with severe punishment, or our holy religion will be held in disrespect."

"Undoubtedly Captain Beauport escaped with too lenient a sentence," said the governor, "though probably the vengeance of heaven has overtaken him ere this: he and all on board the ship in which he sailed are beneath the ocean."

"Because one has escaped, are other criminals to go unpunished?" exclaimed the priest who had before spoken. "Death by shooting or hanging would be too mild a sentence: he deserves the stake, unless by confessing his fault and abjuring his errors he returns to the loving bosom of our holy Church."

Similar remarks were made by the other priest in a manner not usual in a court of law. For some time this mockery of a trial went on. Nigel prayed for strength, for he felt how greatly he needed it. He stood calm and apparently unmoved, listening to the abusive remarks of the vindictive priests. No one raised a voice in his favour. There might have been many who felt for him, but they feared to speak. The men who were judging him were also his accusers. Still he felt bound to defend himself, although he knew full well that the most able defence would not avail him. He pleaded that, with regard to reading the Bible, he was a foreigner and was but doing what was allowed in his own country; that he was not even attempting to make proselytes, and was simply obeying the command of his Lord to search the Scriptures. And that, as to the second accusation, whether or not he approved of what had been done, had he acted otherwise and interfered, he would have been guilty of an infraction of naval discipline; therefore he could not be made answerable for what had been done.

"He acknowledges himself guilty of sacrilege, for ecclesiastical law is above all other law, and that would have compelled him to interfere," cried the priest. "Death, death, to the heretic!" and several voices echoed the savage cry.

"You are undoubtedly guilty of the crime alleged against you, Monsieur Lieutenant," said the governor, after consulting in an undertone with the two priests at his side. "Your being a foreigner, as you are in the service of France, will not avail you. You will have two days given you to consider whether you will recant, and if not, your sentence is 'That you be bound to a stake, with fire kindled around you till your body is consumed, and your soul is carried off by the emissaries of Satan, who are certainly waiting for it.'"

Nigel listened calmly while the governor was pronouncing his terrible doom—one to which the Church of Rome had already condemned tens of thousands of human beings for simply reading the Bible.

Without being allowed to say another word, he was seized by the guards waiting the beck of the governor, and dragged out of the court. Instead, however, of being led back to the prison where he had previously been confined, he found that he was actually leaving the fort. The governor was, in truth, afraid to keep him there, for a considerable number of the *Madeline's* crew, who were much attached to him, were doing duty on shore, and, although they attended the Romish service, he was well aware that still in their hearts they were Protestants, and he feared that they might rescue him and assist in his escape.

The priests had of late erected close to the church a small building which they intended should serve as an inquisitorial prison where they might keep in confinement any heretics on whom they were desirous of expending their religious zeal. To this place Nigel was taken, and thrust into one of its dungeons built especially under the priests' directions. It was, in truth, little better than a pit dug in the ground, with a small aperture towards the roof to admit light. On this occasion they had obtained a party of soldiers from the governor to guard their prison.

Nigel had not been long shut up in this dreadful place when night came on, and he was left in total darkness, with only a bundle of dry grass on which to lie down and rest himself. Brave as he was, he could not but look forward with painful feelings to the fate prepared for him. He thought, however, more of his young wife and the poor count. He feared, too, that the hatred of the priests might drag them into the same fate. Perhaps even now they were seized and accused of crimes for which their tyrannical oppressors might condemn them to death. Sleep was impossible, while the darkness prevented him from pacing up and down his narrow cell, which would have been some relief to his tortured mind. He felt for the pile of grass and lay down, considering that it would be wiser to try and obtain some rest to prepare himself for the future trials he would have to go through. The sudden destruction of all his happiness, separation from his beloved Constance, and the agonizing death speedily to overtake him, made him have recourse to prayer to obtain that strength ever awarded to those who seek it from on high.

Nigel had been sleeping for some time, when, suddenly awaking, he became conscious that some one was in the vault, by hearing a footstep and a low sound of breathing. A feeling of horror for a moment ran through him. Could it be an assassin sent by the governor or priests to put him secretly to death, and so to save themselves from carrying out the sentence passed on him, from which even they might shrink, aware of the horror it would create among the greater number of the colonists, who, not having been educated in their school, would, whatever their religious sentiments, look at it with disapprobation. Still, for himself it would matter nothing, except being deprived of a few hours of life, and he would thus be saved from the tortures of the flames. Such thoughts rapidly passed through his mind; but in another moment he had nerved himself, like a brave man, to meet whatever might occur. His very natural feeling was to struggle desperately with his supposed assassin. He might even gain the victory and thus make his escape. Full of youth and strength, he felt that it would be better far to die struggling bravely, should the guard set upon him, than to sink down tamely where he lay. Springing to his feet, he stood with his arms prepared for defence.

"Hush!" said a voice. "I thought you were still sleeping. Make no noise—give me your hand and come quickly; there is not a moment to lose."

Nigel knew by the voice and the mode of expression that it was the Indian Cora who spoke. He put out his hand and felt it grasped by her small and delicate fingers. To his surprise he found himself led almost instantly into a narrow passage, with room sufficient only for one person to pass through at a time.

"Stoop low," said Cora, as she conducted him into apparently a small alcove on one side. "Step back and remain a moment," she added, disengaging her hand, immediately after which he heard a grating sound as if a heavy stone were being moved.

Quickly returning, she again took his hand, and led him down a slope of some feet, and then again along a level; when once more they ascended another slope, at the top of which, mounting a few steps, he found himself standing in the open air, surrounded by a thick grove, beyond which he could distinguish the wooden tower of the church. Once more Cora desired him to remain, while she was engaged in closing up the aperture through which they had emerged. Putting her finger on her lips to enforce silence, she once more led him forward at a rapid rate, keeping under the shelter of the trees; where the gloom was such that he could not possibly by himself have made his way. At length they reached a small beach with low cliffs on either side. Keeping under their shade they proceeded till he discovered a canoe concealed beneath a rock. Cora, without requiring his assistance, quickly launched it, and then again taking his hand, bade him, in a whisper, step in and lie down his length at the bottom. Instantly grasping a paddle, she began to make her way rapidly from the shore. She had not got far, when a voice from the cliff hailed, ordering the canoe immediately to come back. Cora took no notice, but paddled on with renewed efforts. Again the person on the cliff shouted, and threatened to fire if his orders were not obeyed. A few seconds only had passed when a shot whistled close to the canoe. Cora bravely paddled on. The man on the cliff must have reloaded quickly, for soon afterwards another shot came, but happily without touching the canoe. The darkness must have soon hid so small an object from the soldier's sight, though the shore was still visible. A third and fourth shot followed, but still wider of the mark. Cora did not relax her efforts till they had got more than half way across the harbour. She then stopped for a moment to listen, but no sound of oars indicated that they were pursued.

"We are safe now," she said, "and you may raise yourself; but don't attempt to stand up. Thankful I am that we have escaped. I have no fear for myself, but I dreaded every moment lest you might have been retaken by your cruel enemies. My brother gave me the task to do, and I gladly accepted it. He himself has gone to summon our tribe to arms, having resolved to rescue you by force had my undertaking failed."

"I am most grateful to you," said Nigel. "But by what wonderful means were you able to enter my prison and liberate me without apparent difficulty?"

"By means which these cruel priests themselves afforded," answered Cora. "When they were building their prison-house, Tecumah and I happened to pass that way and observed that they were placing it on the ground once occupied by an ancient temple at which, in days gone by, our tribe were wont to worship. One of our medicine-men, who had listened to the truth from Tecumah's mouth, told us that there were several passages running underground which had possibly been undiscovered by the builders. He is a sagacious man, and, finding that the new building was intended for a prison, advised us to visit the ancient passage and endeavour to keep it concealed, so that a way might be made if necessary into the dungeon. 'The whites treat us at present with respect,' he observed; 'but the time may come when they may act towards us as the Portuguese have long been acting towards the Indians in their neighbourhood, imprisoning and murdering those who refuse to adopt their faith.' My brother accordingly, with several other young men, led by the medicine-man, paid numerous visits, at night, to the place, unknown to the French. It was thus discovered that an underground passage was being formed between some of the cells of the prison and the church. Fortunately this was found out before the old passage was cut through, and by placing a large stone, turning on a sort of hinge, on one side, they were able to secure a way into the new passage without betraying the existence of their own. By constantly being on the watch, they ascertained that only one cell had as yet been formed into which the passage led. I had resolved when you were made prisoner to attempt your rescue even from the fort; but when I found that you were carried to the priests' prison my hopes of success arose. I had one night, from curiosity, gone with my brother to visit the spot. We then discovered that the door which led into your prison had no lock, but was merely closed with smooth sliding bolts. I thus knew my way, and was able to set you free."

Nigel had no doubt that the object of the passage was to enable the priests either to work on the minds of the prisoners by pretended miraculous appearances; or else, should they desire to murder one of their captives, to convey the body secretly away. He, indeed, knew that such arrangements were common throughout Europe, and that numberless impostures had thus been carried out.

They quickly reached the shore, which had of late been entirely deserted by the Tamoyos, who had, influenced by what had been told them by Tecumah, moved some distance further inland. Cora, who feared that the direction they had taken would be suspected by the French, when Nigel's escape was discovered, advised that they should go forward till he was safe among her tribe.

Dark as the night was, she knew her way, and, light and active, she led him forward at a rapid rate. They had gone some distance, when she exclaimed, "Here come my brother and his people. They will indeed rejoice to find you free."

Nigel was welcomed by Tecumah and his party. They were on their way to the shore, intending immediately to cross, and hoping before daylight to reach the prison. Tecumah, in his anxiety to save Nigel, had induced his followers to swear that they would rescue him by force if they could succeed in no other way. Their intention was to attack the guards and break open the prison, expecting to get off again before the governor and his people had time to pursue them. Nigel assured them how thankful he was that they had not been compelled to resort to such a proceeding. Too probably the governor and priests would wreak their vengeance on his wife and father-in-law. As it was, he felt very anxious as to what would happen when his escape was discovered. It would certainly baffle the sagacity of the priests to ascertain how it had been accomplished, and would undoubtedly make them more savage, as they might naturally

IMPRISONMENT AND RESCUE. 175

suspect that some of their own followers had proved treacherous, and yet not know whom to accuse.

"They shall not injure the count or any of our friends," exclaimed Tecumah. "We can distinguish between the true men and the bad. The last, as God's Word tells us, are always the most numerous, and it shall be our care to defend the innocent and weaker ones. My people shall remain ready with their canoes to cross over at a moment's notice, while I go to the island and learn what has taken place."

Nigel expressed his wish to accompany the Tamoyos, but both Tecumah and Cora urged him to proceed to a further distance, as, should the governor suspect where he had gone, he would in all probability send an expedition over to bring him back, and as they would refuse to give him up, an open rupture would be the consequence. Nigel at last agreed to accompany Cora to her father's abode, which was above five miles from the shore of the harbour, while Tecumah carried out his proposed project.

Leaving his people encamped on the shore with their canoes ready to embark, he paddled across towards the island. He was well aware of the risk he was running, for the governor, should he suspect that he had been instrumental in rescuing Nigel, would in all probability seize him and shut him up in prison. He had taken the precaution, however, of charging the next chief in common after him to come across and demand his liberation.

Daylight broke as he reached the place at which he was accustomed to land. He proceeded at once to the house of the count, who was already on foot, and he had the satisfaction of giving him tidings of Nigel's safety.

"The knowledge that he is free will restore life to my poor daughter," said the count. "But we are still in the power of the governor and those revengeful priests, and I fear much that they will not allow us long to remain in quiet."

"Then come over and live with us!" exclaimed Tecumah. "We will build a house for you and hunt for you, and do our utmost to enable you to live as you are now doing."

"We cannot be thus burdensome to you; and we should have no means of paying your people for labouring in our service," answered the count. "Still, I am most grateful to you, and will think over the matter."

Constance came out of her room as soon as she had risen to thank Tecumah, who then, hoping that his friends would not be interfered with, went on to see the minister.

He had been there for some time, and was about to return, when one of the count's servants rushed into the house, out of breath from running.

"Sad news, Monsieur Laporte!" he explained. "Just ten minutes ago one of those ill-conditioned priests, with half a dozen ruffians of soldiers, came to my master's house and carried him and Madame Nigel off on an accusation of having assisted Monsieur Nigel to escape, and of reading the Bible. What will they do with them? They say Monsieur Nigel was

IMPRISONMENT AND RESCUE. 177

condemned to be burnt, and they will burn them in revenge;" and the poor fellow wrung his hands and burst into tears.

"God will protect them, though I don't see how," said the minister. "Alas! alas! These persecutors of ours have already put many innocent persons to death, and will not scruple to destroy all those who oppose them."

"They must not be allowed to suffer," exclaimed Tecumah, when he heard what had occurred. "I will away to my people before they can stop me; and we will one and all perish before we allow a hair of their heads to be injured."

"I would seek to avoid bloodshed, and must urge you, my friend, to try peaceable measures *first*," said Monsieur Laporte.

"We will endeavour, at all events, to rescue the innocent. You, my friend, come with me; you are in danger here, for they will assuredly seize you," said the Indian, taking the minister's hand.

"I must remain at the post where duty calls me," answered Monsieur Laporte. "I may be the means of leading some perishing soul to turn to God, and should I be imprisoned with my friends I may be a comfort to them. But bear my love and blessing to Nigel, should I be destined never again to see him."

At length Tecumah, finding that the minister was firm, set off, keeping himself concealed as much as possible among the trees, and made his way to his canoe. He had scarcely pushed off from the shore, when he saw several people rushing down to the beach. They had, he guessed rightly, been sent to capture him. There was no boat near at hand or they would have pursued him, though had they done so, his light canoe would quickly have left them astern.

On landing, he found his father and several other chiefs. He narrated to them what had occurred, but, greatly to his disappointment, he found that they objected to do anything which might put an end to the peaceable terms on which they had hitherto lived with the French. They had seen how the Portuguese treated the Indians who opposed them, and they dreaded, they said, the vengeance of the white men.

Tecumah was indignant. The white men who now were in the ascendency were no longer deserving of their friendship, he argued. By treachery and deceit they had overcome those who were their proper leaders, and they were even now about to put them to a cruel death. Tuscarora was grieved that his son's friends should suffer; but he could not for their sakes risk the safety of his tribe. Again Tecumah addressed them with all the eloquence of which he was master. "If," he observed, "they were treacherous towards their own people, they would surely be more likely to ill-treat their dark-skinned allies should it at any time be to their interest to do so, and it would be better to strike a blow at once and prevent them from doing harm, rather than allow them, after they had cut off all those who were worthy of confidence, to destroy us." Tecumah saw that he was winning many to his side, and persevered. At length one of the chiefs proposed that he should be allowed to go over with a select body of men, and rescue the prisoners.

To this Tuscarora agreed, and Tecumah was obliged to content himself with this plan, trusting that no harm would be done in the mean time to the count and his daughter.

Some hours had passed when, as Tecumah was eagerly waiting on the beach for the moment fixed for the expedition to set out, he saw a canoe paddling down the harbour. He recognized it as one of those sent up the estuary to keep watch and to give timely notice of the approach of an enemy. As the occupant leapt on shore, he exclaimed—

"Haste! haste! The Portuguese and Tuparas, and several other tribes in alliance with them, are on the war-path. They have hundreds of canoes, and they will soon after nightfall attack the island unless they first land and try to destroy us."

CHAPTER XI.

CAPTURE OF THE FORT.

CONSTANCE and her father, rudely dragged from their home, were hurried off to the fort. No allowance was made for the weakness of her sex, and no pity was shown her by the savage priests, who, supposing that she was not aware of her husband's escape, endeavoured still more to wound her feelings by telling her that he was condemned to death, and that, unless she and her father recanted, they would meet with the same fate.

"Silence, priest, silence! It is cowardly and unmanly to speak thus to my daughter," exclaimed the count. "Add not insult to the injury you have already inflicted. We have broken no laws; we have done harm to no one; and we find ourselves treated as if we were the vilest of malefactors."

The count's address had no effect upon the priest, who took a cruel pleasure in annoying them. Such is ever the character of the emissaries of Rome when they are in the ascendency and are opposed; when in the minority, they are humble and meek, plausible and silver-tongued; and when there are none to oppose them, haughty, indolent, sensual, and self-indulgent. Such they have been in all ages and in every country, with the exception of the devoted Jesuit slaves, who have gone forth to carry their spurious gospel into heathen lands.

On arriving at the fort, the mockery of a trial was gone through; the priest's myrmidons swore to having seen Constance reading the Bible, and that, as the crime had been committed on the count's property, he was therefore equally guilty. Having been a lawyer in his youth, the count was able to defend himself, and had a jury of twelve honest men been present, he would have undoubtedly been acquitted; but, unhappily, that system being unknown among the French, he had no such advantage. The governor and the priest, exasperated at Nigel's escape, grossly abused him, and interrupted him with shouts and execrations whenever he especially pointed to the proofs of his innocence. The count, of course, defended Constance, and argued that she was but listening to her husband, whom she was bound to obey, and was therefore guiltless.

"It is false!" exclaimed the priest, starting up;

"her duty to the Church is above all others. It was for her to denounce her husband rather than to listen to him. Such heretical notions as yours, Count de Tourville, must be destroyed. The Church would lose her authority and power were they to prevail."

"Ma foi!" exclaimed the count; "in that case no husband can venture to trust his wife with the slightest secret. It would not be confided to her keeping, but to that of the confessor. For that reason, and many others, we repudiate the system you, for your own ends, are anxious to maintain. I advise those who are husbands never to tell to their wives words they would not have known where the system prevails."

"Silence! Count de Tourville," exclaimed the priest, foaming with rage, "you shall answer for these insulting words."

The count, it must be confessed, regretted having touched on the subject, as it was like throwing pearls to swine; but he felt for the moment that he might shield his daughter by drawing the anger of the priests on himself.

The mockery of a trial came to a conclusion, and the governor, who had taken upon himself the office of judge and inquisitor-general, found the count and his daughter guilty of the crimes with which they were charged, and condemned them both to death. In consequence of Nigel's escape, the priest begged that they might be kept for safe custody in the prison within the fort; the same wretched place in which Nigel had first been confined, and utterly unfit for the reception of any female. Poor Constance shuddered as she was led into it. Her father begged that he might send to his house for such necessaries as his daughter required, but his request was roughly refused. It was not without difficulty even that he obtained some matting, and a few armfuls of rushes on which she might rest.

"Lie down, my child," said the count to Constance, when they were at length left alone. "We will not altogether despair, but look to Him who is always ready to protect us. You require rest; and we know not what we may have to go through."

Constance obeyed her father, while he continued pacing up and down the narrow space allowed him, to collect his thoughts. He harboured no ill-feeling towards his persecutors, but, following the example of his Master, he prayed for their forgiveness, while he looked forward with joy, rather than fear, to the time when he should be welcomed into His presence. He knew, too, that his beloved daughter, should her life be taken, would bear him company to that home where their Saviour had gone before to prepare a place for all those who love Him.

The night passed on. Constance was sleeping. Still the count felt no desire to lie down and rest. The whole fort seemed wrapped in silence, except when the voice of a distant sentry reached his ear. The silence was suddenly broken by a shot fired from the fort. Others followed in rapid succession. Then arose loud shouts and shrieks, and the Indian warwhoop rising above all others. Constance started from her slumbers, and clung to her father. The noises grew louder and louder.

"The fort is attacked. The enemy are scaling the walls!" exclaimed the count. "Both parties are fighting desperately. Constance, there is hope for us, for even the Portuguese would scarcely wish to injure those who are unable to oppose them."

The sounds of strife increased. The count could with difficulty judge how the fight was going. Supporting his daughter on his arm, he awaited the issue. The great guns roared, the bullets rattled, and presently there came an uproar which showed that the assailants had gained the fort, and the shriek and cries of the combatants, and other sounds of a desperate struggle, approached their prison. Just at that juncture the warwhoops of apparently a fresh party burst forth within the fort. The count recognized the cry as that of the Tamoyos. On they came from the opposite side of the fort, and the battle seemed to rage hotter than ever. In the midst of the fierce turmoil the door of their prison was burst open, and Tecumah, leaping in, seized Constance in his arms, while a companion took charge of the count, and hurried him off.

"I promised to save you or perish," said the Indian. "We had a hard matter to enter the fort, and it will be no less difficult to escape; but I have succeeded thus far, and trust to place you in safety."

These words were uttered hurriedly, as Tecumah, surrounded by a faithful band, was fighting his way across the fort, in all parts of which a furious battle

THE FLIGHT.

CAPTURE OF THE FORT. 187

was raging; the Portuguese and their Indian allies, the Tuparas, having forced an entrance, being engaged with the French and Tamoyos, who were struggling desperately for life.

Bullets were whizzing and arrows flying in all directions; the fierce shouts and shrieks of the combatants sounding above the clash of steel and the rattle of musketry. Numbers and discipline favoured the Portuguese, who had well trained their native allies, while the French mistrusted each other, and had but little confidence in the natives, who, however, were gallantly doing their utmost to assist them, headed by their brave chief, Tuscarora. Tecumah and his faithful band had but one object in view, to rescue Constance and her father. Like a wedge, with their most stalwart warriors in the van, they fought their way through the mass of foes entering the fort towards the outlet which had allowed the latter ingress. Several of their number fell; scarcely one escaped a wound. Still Constance was untouched. Often they were almost overwhelmed. Still on they went, their track marked by the bodies of their foes, and many of their own party. The gateway was reached. Constance felt Tecumah stagger. A fear seized her that he had received a wound; but no cry escaped him, and, recovering himself, he bore her onwards. Scarcely had they emerged into the open, when they encountered a fresh party of the Portuguese. The Tamoyos halted for a moment to draw their bows, and not a shaft failed to pierce a foe, the shower of bullets, which came in return, passing mostly over their heads.

"On! on!" shouted Tecumah, though his voice no longer rang with its usual clear tone.

Constance observed with grief that he was faint and hoarse. His band, obeying him, turned round and shot their arrows as they advanced. Scarcely, however, had they moved forward, when the Portuguese, seeing the handful of men opposed to them, fiercely charged their ranks, Tecumah and only a few of the warriors surrounding him, having got some way in advance, escaping the onslaught; the rest, who had the count in charge, were compelled to halt, in a vain endeavour to withstand their overwhelming foes. The darkness enabled Tecumah, and the few who remained by him, to push on without being observed.

"On! on!" again cried Tecumah. "The rest will follow when they have driven back our enemies."

"Oh, my father! my father! Where is he?" exclaimed Constance.

Tecumah did not answer her.

Making their way towards the shore, they reached it at length.

"Where are the canoes?" exclaimed Tecumah, looking along the beach where they had been left hauled up.

His companions dispersed on either side to look for them. Their cries told what had happened. Some had been sent adrift, and others had been battered in, and utterly destroyed by a band of Tuparas, as the Tamoyos truly surmised.

"We must make our way to the spot where they

CAPTURE OF THE FORT.   189

have left their canoes," exclaimed Tecumah; and he again attempted to lift up Constance, who had earnestly entreated to be placed on the ground.

The din of battle still sounded as loud as ever, and the rattle of musketry was heard close at hand. It was evident that the combatants were approaching the shore.

"On! on!" again cried Tecumah; and, lifting up Constance, he was staggering forward, when, faint from loss of blood, he sank on the ground.

At that moment an Indian rushed out of the wood behind them. "Fly! fly! our enemies are at hand. All, all have been cut to pieces. I alone have escaped."

His arm, as he spoke, dropped by his side, while the blood flowed rapidly from his head, giving evidence of the truth of his assertion.

Constance was kneeling down, trying to staunch the blood flowing from Tecumah's wound. He raised himself on one arm.

"Think not of me," he said, "but endeavour, with my faithful friends, who will accompany you, to find concealment among the rocks."

"We cannot leave you," answered Constance; "better to yield ourselves prisoners, than to allow you to perish alone."

"You know not the nature of our enemies," said Tecumah, faintly; "they spare no one. Fly, fly, while there is time."

The sounds of fighting were drawing rapidly nearer. All prospect of escape seemed cut off. Constance gazed up for a moment from the task at which she was engaged. Bullets were striking the branches of the trees a short distance from them. Her heart sank with grief. She felt the probability that her father had been cut off with the rest of the brave Tamoyos. Just then one of the Indians exclaimed, "See, see! a canoe approaches." Constance cast a glance across the waters, and caught a glimpse of a canoe emerging from the darkness. It rapidly approached the beach. The shouts of the Indians showed that friends were on board. Their hails were answered. In another moment Nigel leapt on shore. Tecumah recognized him.

"Save her first—care not for me," he exclaimed.

Nigel was not likely to disobey such a command, and, taking Constance in his arms, he bore her to the canoe.

"Oh, save our brave friend," she cried, as she pressed her lips to her husband's, who immediately sprang back to the beach, and, listening not to Tecumah's request to be allowed to die where he lay, he carried him, with the assistance of the Indians who still had strength to exert themselves, to the canoe.

Holding the steering paddle in her hands, stood Cora. The instant her brother and Nigel were on board, she gave it a dexterous turn, and the canoe shot away from the shore, impelled by the strokes of two lads who formed the crew. Nigel and an Indian seized two other paddles, and with all their strength urged on the canoe. There was no time to be lost; already they could see a number of dark forms emerging from the wood, while numerous bullets splashed into the water astern. The veil of night would prove their best protection, and every effort was made to get ahead. Cora, believing that they could no longer be seen, directed the canoe on a different course, to one side parallel with the shore, thus avoiding the bullets which were fired in the direction it had last been seen. After going on for some distance, she again steered directly for the opposite shore, which her keen sight could distinguish through the darkness. Meantime, Constance, seated at the bottom of the canoe, supported Tecumah's head. He gently took her hand, and pressed it to his lips.

"I have more to thank you for than I can express by words," he whispered, in a low, faltering voice. "I first followed a shadow, but you showed me the glorious reality, and led me to Him, whom to know is life eternal. I die happy, resting in His love, with the thought also that I have preserved your life to be a blessing to one who is worthy of you. I am going quickly, but do not mourn aloud, lest you paralyse the efforts of our friends."

Constance felt the hand which held hers relax its grasp, and ere long she knew that the spirit of the young Indian had taken its flight to the realms of bliss. She placed his hand on his breast, and, obeying his dying injunctions, refrained from giving way to her feelings. Not till they were near the north shore, and safe for the present from their enemies, did she speak. She then endeavoured to prepare Cora for the discovery of her brother's death.

"I feared it was so," replied Cora, when Constance had told her clearly what had happened. "I know, however, that no joy on earth could be more exquisite than that he felt in the consciousness that he had given his life to save yours. I must not mourn for him as those who have no hope. We must not remain here," continued Cora, as they disembarked from the canoe. "They will certainly pursue us, and we shall not be in safety till we reach our village, where the remnant of our tribe is collected. Alas! there will be bitter grief and loud wailing for the many who have, I fear, fallen."

With perfect calmness Cora gave directions to her people to convey the body of her brother, and follow quickly, while she led Nigel, who supported Constance, through the woods. Faint and overcome with grief as Constance was, Cora urged, notwithstanding, that they should continue their course without stopping, for she felt convinced that a fearful loss had overtaken her tribe from the account which the last-arrived Indian had given her. He had, he affirmed, before Tecumah and his party had cut their way out of the fort, seen Tuscarora and many of their tribe shot down by the enemy; and he had also witnessed the death of the count. Nigel questioned him narrowly, but could elicit nothing that could shake his testimony.

Sad, indeed, as Cora had expected, was the way in which they were received at her village, and it was feared, indeed, that even it might be attacked while there only remained the old men and boys for its defence. It was proposed, therefore, that they should move further into the country; but Cora urged them to remain, and, as a precaution against surprise, sent out scouts to give timely notice of the appearance of an enemy, or the return of their friends. They all, however, packed up their property, and remained prepared for instant flight.

CHAPTER XII.

CONCLUSION.

JUST as dawn was breaking, a warrior was seen approaching the village. His bow was broken; his dress torn and besmeared with blood. The inhabitants, who were on the watch, anxiously went out to meet him. He hung down his head without uttering a word, and not for some time could he be induced to speak. At length, a groan bursting from his breast, he exclaimed—

"All, all, are lost! In vain our warriors, led by Tuscarora, fought to the last. One after another they were shot down by the bullets of the white faces, or cut to pieces by the war hatchets of the hated Tuparas. Our French allies, deserting the fort, fought their way to their boats, and, embarking, fled to their ships, leaving us to our fate. Two only with myself escaped by leaping over the walls, and swimming to a canoe floating by. Both of my companions were wounded. As we were paddling on, as fast as our strength would allow, we caught sight of a canoe with two Portuguese boats in pursuit. We were unobserved, but we had too much reason to fear that the canoe was overtaken. Just as we reached the shore, the paddles dropped from the hands of my two companions, and they sank down from loss of blood. When I called to them, they gave no answer. They were both dead. I waited in vain for the arrival of our friends, but none appeared, and I at length came on to bring the sad tidings."

As the wounded warrior finished his narrative, loud wailings rose from the women in the camp. No threats of vengeance were uttered, for they felt their utter helplessness, and they knew that they themselves might become the prey of any of their foes who might be induced to attack them. At length an old man arose in their midst.

"Give not way to despair, my daughters," he exclaimed; "you have still many sons. We will fly with them to a place of safety, and there teach them how their brave fathers fought and died with their faces to the foe. They will grow up, and, hearing of their deeds, will imitate their valour, and revenge the deaths of their sires."

The words of the aged warrior restored the drooping courage of the poor women, and they resolved to follow his counsel. A few men, who from sickness or other causes had not gone forth to battle, and the youths who had not sufficient strength to draw their mighty bows, vowed to defend them and the chief's daughter to the last gasp. Cora deputed the old warrior to take the lead, and, as they believed the Tuparas, flushed with victory, would ere long pursue them, they immediately set out on their sad journey to the north.

Surrounding Nigel and Constance, they vowed fidelity, promising to obey the last behests of their beloved young chief Tecumah, and to afford them all the support in their power. A small band only of the bravest and most active remained behind to collect any stragglers who might arrive, and to cover the retreat of the main body. Nigel, communicating with the old chief, found that he proposed proceeding northward to a region bordering the sea, inhabited by a scanty tribe, with whom the Tamoyos were on friendly terms, the former having been driven from their own hunting-grounds by a more powerful tribe. This intelligence was satisfactory to Nigel and Constance, as they thus had hopes of being able to communicate with some English or French ship which might appear off the shore.

The spot to which the Tamoyos were directing their course was at length gained. It was a deep wide valley, surrounded by rugged hills, and could not be approached towards the sea except by a narrow gorge, which could be defended by a few brave men, who could lie concealed among the rocks, and hurl down stones on the heads of invaders. The Indians carried with them, as was their custom, cuttings and roots of fruit trees and plants, which they had cultivated in their native district. Without loss of time, they began erecting huts and laying out plantations, the old men and women being generally employed in such occupations, while the young men went out hunting, they having at present to depend on the produce of the chase for their subsistence. The tribe showed the greatest attention to Nigel and Constance, whom they considered committed to their care by their beloved young chief, doing their utmost to secure their comfort and convenience. Indeed, they treated them with the same respect they bestowed on Cora, who was now the acknowledged chieftainess of the tribe. They built a cottage after the model of those they had seen on the island, and laid out a garden, which they planted with fruit trees and vegetables. Nigel and his wife in return, aided by Cora, instructed them in Gospel truth. They also taught them, as far as they had the means, the arts of civilized life. Thus the days went rapidly by. Still, though the young couple enjoyed much happiness, they could not help wishing to return to Europe, while they often thought, with grief, of the loss of the count and of their other beloved friend.

Besides the account brought by the Indian who escaped from the fort, they could gain no further tidings of their fate. Nigel would, had he had himself only to consider, have set out to try and ascertain what had become of the colony, but he could not bring himself to leave Constance, even though he had full confidence in the fidelity of their Indian friends. Cora, to whom Constance expressed Nigel's wishes, at length promised to send out a scout, who would endeavour to find out what had happened. Nigel gladly accepted Cora's offer.

Nearly a month had passed since the scout set out, and fears were entertained that he had perished. At last, however, one evening, he was seen descending the side of the hill, along the steep and difficult path by which, as has been said, the valley could alone be reached from the southward; he was accompanied by a white man, whose tottering steps he supported in the difficult descent. As they approached the village, the gaunt form and haggard features of the latter prevented Nigel, who went out to meet them, from recognizing him.

"You don't know me, Monsieur Lieutenant; I am Jacques Baville, whom you knew well as a true Protestant. I assisted the escape of our good minister, Laporte, who was committed to the care of some of the brave Indians by the young chief Tecumah. We fought our way to the water's side, and embarked in a canoe; but before we had got far, we were chased by two of the enemy's boats, and captured. We expected instant death, but were reserved for a more cruel fate. We were conveyed to the south shore, where we heard that the forts on the island had all been destroyed, and our countrymen, with the traitor Villegagnon, had sailed away, leaving most of the Protestants to the cruel vengeance of our foes. To commemorate their victory, the Portuguese had resolved, we found, on building a city. One of the first edifices erected was a prison, into which the good minister and several other persons were thrown; while the Tamoyos, who had been taken prisoners, with two other artisans, like myself, were employed, with many people of other tribes, who had been reduced to slavery by the Portuguese, in labouring at the work going forward. A church was next built, and filled full of idols for the people to worship. As soon as it was finished, the minister and other captives were led from the prison, and dragged into it, when they were ordered to worship, as the other people were doing. They refused, however, to bow their heads to the saints, or other false gods, but stood motionless, with their arms folded. The priests, on this, reviled them, and threatened them with death if they refused. Still they were firm, declaring that they would not mock God with such senseless ceremonies. On this they were taken back to prison; and we, seeing how they behaved, resolved to imitate them. Several times they were carried before the priests, who sat in the church to try them for what was called their heresy. The trial was still going on when two priests arrived, who declared they had been on board a Portuguese ship, bringing over numerous images and relics and indulgences to St. Vincente, when she was captured by a French man-of-war, the captain of which had sacrilegiously thrown them into the sea. I, of course, knew that they spoke of the *Madeline;* and, as you remember, Monsieur Lieutenant, I was on board, I began to fear that I might be recognized. Monsieur Laporte, of course, stated that he was not there, and could, therefore, not be considered guilty of the act of which they complained, supposing that it had taken place. The priests, however, who were eager to find some one on whom to wreak their vengeance, declared that it mattered nothing, even had he not been there, as the act was performed by those of his faith, and was the result of the pernicious doctrines he taught. He defended himself nobly, but was condemned to be burnt alive in the centre of a wide spot, which had been marked out for a square.

"Hoping that I had not been recognized by the priests, I was making my way out of the church, when the keen eyes of one of them fell on me. He instantly ordered me to be seized, and at once declared that he had seen me on board the *Madeline*, engaged in throwing the trumpery overboard. I would not deny this, but said that I was but doing my duty, and obeying my captain, and that, had he ordered me to throw the two priests themselves overboard, to look after their saints, I should certainly have done so. This enraged them more than ever, and they threatened to burn me with the minister. As I was, however, known to be a good carpenter, the civil officers were not willing to lose my services, and I was sent back to prison.

"In vain they tried to make the good minister recant. He refused to do so. They promised him his life and full pardon, and a good post under government, but he refused all their offers, saying that he would rather die a hundred deaths than abandon the faith of the pure gospel. The next day he was led to the place of execution. We were compelled to be present. The faggots were piled round him. Some of the people, moved with pity, cried out that he should be strangled first, and the executioner himself seemed unwilling to light the pile; when one of the priests, seizing the torch, set fire to the faggots, which quickly blazed up, and our good minister's soul went to that happy home prepared for him. The priests, having caught sight of me, insisted that I should be thrown into prison to await their pleasure, which I knew very well would be ere long to burn me at the stake.

"Some of our countrymen, I am sorry to say, recanted, and were set free, but others held fast. I determined, however, if I could, to make my escape, should I have strength enough to do so; for we were so poorly fed that I expected, before long, to be starved. All the prisoners had hitherto been confined in a common cell; but after I was condemned, I was placed in one by myself. It was in a new part of the prison, which I had actually been employed in building. The whole structure was of wood, though, at the same time, very strong. I knew that I could not make my way through the walls, nor underground, as the stakes were driven down deep, and no human strength could force them up; but I recollected the way I had put on the roof; and, though the slabs were heavy, I was certain that I could force one of them up sufficiently to allow me to get through. I had not been long shut up, when a priest came, and endeavoured to make me recant, picturing the horrible tortures I should suffer in this world, and in the next, if I refused. I asked him whence he got his authority. He answered from the Church. I replied that the Bible was before the Church; and that the Bible says, 'Whosoever believeth on Me shall not perish, but have everlasting life;' and that, though he might burn my body, Christ could save my soul. He replied that the Bible must not be interpreted by laymen, and that the Church had alone the power to explain it. I observed that the Church of Christ had ever explained it exactly as I did, and to that Church I belonged; that the system which he called 'The Church,' was built up at Rome by pagan priests, and had ever since been employed in adding falsehood to falsehood, for the sake of imposing on the minds of the people, and compelling them to do their will; and that, if he wished to serve Christ, he must leave his false church, as thousands of my countrymen had done, and tens of thousands in Germany and England, or that he himself would perish eternally. Without saying another word, he left the cell, and I felt pretty sure would not come back again.

"I had a sheath knife, which I had managed to conceal inside my trousers, and immediately set to work, and wrenched up a stool fixed against the wall. There were several nails in it, which I cut out; and then, making a couple of deep notches in one of the angles of the wall, I fixed the bench a certain height below the roof, which enabled me, by standing on it, to force up one of the slabs with my back. Knowing where the nails were driven in, I carefully cut around them, making as little noise as possible. It was, I calculated, about midnight when I had finished my preparations. The slab lifted even more easily than I had expected. I listened for some minutes, expecting to hear the tread of a sentry, but not a sound reached my ears. I had great hopes that he had fallen asleep. Creeping through, I replaced the slab, and dropped without noise to the ground. There were numerous Indians in the camp, many of whom had canoes, for the purpose of fishing. Without loss of time, I crept away, stooping low down, so that, had I been seen, I might be mistaken, in the darkness, for a large dog, or some wild animal prowling about in search of food. I thus, without interruption, made my way down to the shore. There were several canoes hauled up, as I had expected, with paddles left in them. To launch one and to shove off did not occupy much time. The night was dark, but I could make out the opposite shore. With all my might I paddled towards it. On landing, I shoved off the canoe, in the hopes that it would float away, and thus not betray the direction I had taken. Scarcely had I got a hundred yards from the beach, when I encountered this my friend, who conducted me here. I am grieved to bring such tidings, and I fear much that those who remain will be put to death, if they refuse to abandon their faith; and I pray that they may have grace and spirit to continue in it. But I myself must not boast, as I know not what torture and starvation would have led me to do."

Nigel and Constance heard, with deep sorrow, this

account of the martyrdom of their beloved friend and minister; but they were comforted with the knowledge that he had exchanged a life of trial and suffering for a glorious existence in heaven.

Several months passed by. Jacques Baville completely recovered, and was of great assistance in improving their cottage home. He felt, however, even a greater longing than they did to return to his native land.

"Ships may come and go, and we may not see them, unless we are constantly on the watch," he observed. "I have bethought me of building a hut on the height near the shore; and if you, Monsieur Lieutenant, will supply me with food, I will undertake to keep a bright look-out as long as my eyes last me. We will have a flagstaff and flag, and it will not be my fault if we don't manage to communicate with any ship which appears off the coast."

Nigel gladly entered into honest Jacques's plan, and assisted him in building his hut, and putting up a flagstaff. Still week after week passed by, and Jacques had always the same answer to give when Nigel visited him. Nigel himself had ample occupation in cultivating his garden, varied by hunting expeditions with the Indians. He was returning home one evening, when, as he approached his cottage, Constance came running out to meet him. Her agitation would scarcely allow her to speak.

"Come, Nigel, come! I have been longing for your arrival," she exclaimed, taking his hand. "An old friend has arrived, and is waiting to see you."

CONCLUSION.

She led him on, when great was his joy and surprise to see standing in the porch, with outstretched hands, his former commander, Captain Beauport. They entered the cottage, when, sitting down, the captain briefly narrated his history, and the circumstances which had brought him again to the coast of South America. He little expected to find Nigel and Constance alive. Thé crew and passengers of the ship which was conveying him as a prisoner to France, who were all Protestants, had insisted on his liberation; and the commander, who was well-disposed towards him, had, without much difficulty, yielded to their wishes. By great exertions the ships had been kept afloat; and, after enduring severe hardships, had reached Hennebonne, in France. Here the commander, as directed, delivered his despatches to the chief magistrate, who, providentially for the passengers, was a staunch Protestant. On opening them, he found that the traitor, Villegagnon, had denounced them as arch-heretics, worthy of the stake, and advised that they should be immediately delivered up to punishment. The worthy magistrate, indignant at the treachery with which they had been treated, assisted them by every means in his power; while Captain Beauport, knowing that his life would not be safe should he remain in France, immediately embarked on board a vessel bound for England. He there found many Protestant friends, who had fled to escape the fearful persecutions to which they were subjected in France. By their means he obtained the command of an English ship. He had made two or three short voyages, and had, some time before, come out on an exploring expedition to South America, from which he was returning. He was sailing northward, on his way to England, when he observed Jacques Baville's signal.

As may be supposed, Nigel and Constance, with honest Jacques, did not lose the opportunity of returning with him. They parted from Cora with sincere regret.

"It is but natural that you should wish to dwell in your own country, and among your own people," said the Indian girl. "My love makes me wish to accompany you, but my duty compels me to remain with my tribe. On our hearts your images will remain engraved as long as they beat with life."

She, with all her people, attended them to the beach, as they put off towards the ship, which lay at anchor in the harbour. As long as any object was visible on the shore, Cora was seen waving her adieus. The sails were spread to the wind, and the ship glided out into the ocean on her destined course towards the shores of England.

They reached that land of freedom in safety, and Nigel resolved to take up his residence here, with his young wife, rather than expose her to the dangers to which she would be subjected in her native land. He wrote to honest Maître Leroux, who had heard from the count of Constance's marriage, and was ready to pay over to Nigel the rents of the estate.

During the occasional intervals of peace, Nigel paid several visits to Tourville, and, on the death of the steward, sold the estate, and invested the money in an English property, both he and his wife agreeing that it was far better to live on moderate means in a land where they could enjoy the blessings of civil and religious liberty, than in any country under the galling yoke of Papal tyranny.

THE END.